Chris Harvey

The Oxford Illustrated Press

© Chris Harvey and The Oxford Illustrated History Press 1985
Reprinted 1988
Printed in Great Britain by J.H. Haynes & Co Limited

ISBN 0 946609 04 7

Published by;
The Oxford Illustrated Press Limited,
Sparkford, Yeovil, Somerset BA22 7JJ

Haynes Publications Inc
861 Lawrence Drive, Newbury Park,
California 91320 USA

Contents

Acknowledgements

My earliest memories of motoring centred not on my father's Jaguar and M.G., but around a distant relative's Austin Seven deep in the Norfolk countryside. It is difficult to remember what colour the car was, because it was invariably covered in mud and things far worse. I do remember, however, that it was an open model—a Chummy as I realise now—because it was extraordinarily easy to load: he simply threw his hay bales in the back, or roped in whatever livestock he wanted to carry to market. This car also served as a village taxi, collecting people from the station and transporting them up the most awful farm tracks. On special days, doubtless to keep me out of my mother's hair, I was allowed to perch in the front and watch enthralled as this machine was set into motion. But although it had a widespread reputation for never failing to start, it was the stopping of it that was the most fascinating operation: my uncle, or whatever he was, yanked a piece of binder twine that hung beneath the instrument panel, which duly brought the car to a grinding halt. In desperate times, this primitive form of strangulation was brought into effect when the brakes had given up. It also proved well-nigh unstoppable while traversing the most difficult terrain. 'My heart alive, she go through a furrow better than a tractor,' said George with appreciation. Sadly, he is long gone and probably his Austin Seven too, because I left Norfolk when I was only four years old and that was more than forty years ago. But the memories live on to remind me what was an impressive, endearing car the Austin Seven has always been.

All those memories came flooding back when I met Ian Dunford, so long a pillar of the Austin Seven clubs, on a run with a dozen or so of the survivors into the mountains of Wales on a crisp weekend in March. Those club members drove with a rare spirit that was full of the joys of spring, and which made it hard for a modern car to keep up through those twisting lanes. It served especially to remind me how little cars have progressed since the first Austin Seven was built more than sixty years ago. And every time I see one racing today I have to thank Dave Bradley and Ken Cooke of the 750 Motor Club who are as big a mine of information in their scene as Ian is in his. I am truly indebted also to Anders Clausager, of the British Motor Industry Heritage Trust, without whose invaluable support I would be lost; and to that great Austin Seven enthusiast,

Neill Bruce, who, with his wife, Miggie, provided some really memorable photographs; and to my wife, Mary, who shot the Hilton Press Services pictures that I could not. My sincere thanks are also extended to Phil Baildon and Brian Purves of the Austin Seven Clubs' Association for the help they gave so willingly in ensuring the accuracy of the text. Like, mine, it was a labour of love.

For the book itself, I must thank John Haynes, of the Haynes Publishing group, and Jane Marshall, of Oxford Illustrated Press, for unshakeable enthusiasm and, once again, incredible patience in waiting for the completion of a very long job. John, of course, has had the Austin Seven close to his heart since he built his first special as a schoolboy, then wrote about it and published the first book of the thousands that were to follow from Haynes Publishing.

But more than anything, I suppose I should thank that long-suffering Chummy itself! It was the first car I 'drove', clasping the steering wheel as I sat on my Uncle George's lap...

Chris Harvey,
Hethe,
Oxon, August 1988

Colour Plates

I
Austin Seven

Few cars have engendered greater affection than the Austin Seven. This is partly because they were always incredibly cheap (whether new or second-hand) and made in large numbers, which meant that they were often a driver's first car. There were also some amazing quirks which made Austin Sevens easy to drive badly and difficult to drive well. As a result, bad drivers were thrilled to be able to drive it at all and good drivers just as pleased to be able to do it properly. Apart from its great international rival, the Model T Ford, the Austin Seven probably introduced more people to motoring than any other car, decimating the market for motor cycles and sidecars. Austin Sevens were not only a bargain to buy, they

A famous picture ... Sir Herbert Austin looks thoroughly satisfied with his new Seven. It is the earliest known picture of the car, a prototype built in 1922 with a small screen that had no provision for hood fixing points, and used oil lamps and a hand-operated Klaxon horn, probably because it had not yet been wired for electric light!

were very tough and reliable, being made from first-class materials, and subject to excellent quality control. It was with cars like this that the British motor industry established an enviable reputation before the Second World War.

On the other hand, the Austin Seven had its problems: a ride like the rocky road to Dublin, steering that was vague in the extreme, and positively perilous brakes.

Few cars have had more written about them: the Austin Seven has been examined in great detail and it is inevitable that it should have been compared with Peugeot's Quadrilette. Indeed, the first Austin Seven, a single-cylinder car built in 1910, was a copy of the Swift made in the same factory. In much the same way, the Austin Seven as we know it took inspiration from the Peugeot. But it will always be remembered as the car that Herbert Austin pulled out of his hat, as it were, just in time to save his company from bankruptcy.

The first ones appeared in 1922, with production getting under way properly in 1923. These early cars were open tourers, with individual seats like an opened-out bucket at the front, and a bench at the back for children, livestock, or other objects. The cars were called Chummies because the occupants had to be on very good terms to enjoy a trip in it, squashed as they were into a body about three feet square.

The chassis was simplicity itself, like a capital A in lay-out, with two more cross pieces, one of which substituted for the apex, providing a base for the radiator and the front suspension. The absolute minimum of steel was used in

The Austin Seven's chassis was a picture of simplicity with the A-frame extended by quarter elliptic springs at the back and a transverse leaf at the front, braced by diagonal shackles. This chassis was photographed in 1930.

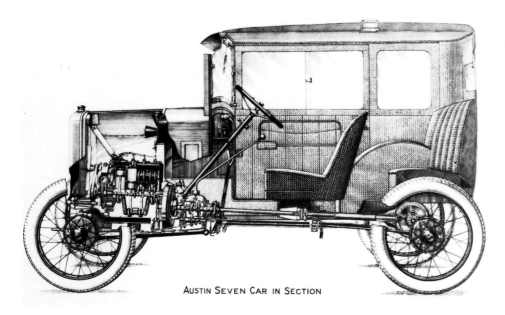

AUSTIN SEVEN CAR IN SECTION

The diminutive size of the Austin Seven's engine and transmission are well illustrated by this sectional drawing of a 1930 model.

this frame, with quarter elliptic springs serving as the rear half. This made the Seven unusually sinuous when it was required to clamber over rough ground. But the lack of rigidity contributed to the most extraordinary handling. The transverse leaf spring at the front had nothing to anchor it against sideways movement, save a couple of shackles. As a result, the car moved from side to side with every bump, making it impossible to hold in a straight line. But if you didn't know any better, which was the case with the majority of motorists who bought an Austin Seven, you just accepted that cars needed constant correction to be kept in rein. Also, when you went round corners, the inside spring at the back flattened as the body rolled, and the outside one arched. The rear axle was held in place additionally by a torque tube in the middle, so it pivotted around this, giving an element of rear-wheel steering. But the driver, unencumbered by any other knowledge of how a car should handle, corrected automatically. The body then rolled the other way and the car carried on with a sort of waltzing motion, which meant that you had to do it all over again until the road straightened up. To be fair to Austin, there were several other cars that handled like this at about that time, notably Citroen's beloved Cloverleaf. Such foibles became part of the charm that was the Austin Seven.

The chassis was extended later to carry larger bodies, and lengthened by half a foot in 1932, which improved the ride a lot.

The first engines were of only 696 cc, but they were soon increased to the definitive 747.5 cc, with a bore of 56 mm. This very narrow measure kept the RAC horsepower rating down to 7.8 and the tax based upon it to only £8 per year: a massive sales attraction in Britain, when it cost £23 a year to tax a Model T Ford, for instance. Fortunately, the long stroke of 76.2 mm which resulted gave the Austin Seven a lot of torque, or chugging ability. The engine was never powerful in standard form, and as a result it lasted a long time.

The Austin Seven rocked and rolled alarmingly, but proved very tenacious when it came to clambering over the most difficult terrain. Ian Dunford drives his 1929 tourer everywhere...

The crankshaft was as eccentric as the construction of the chassis: originally, it was of only 1.125 ins diameter with just two bearings. This meant that the unsupported centre whipped a lot and the main bearings soon started to grumble. But, amazingly, they went on grumbling for thousands of miles with no untoward effect! Other sound effects were provided by the permanently-attached starting handle, which tinkled in time with the crankshaft's vibrations, plus the whirring of the radiator's fan pulley. You drove an Austin Seven as much with your ears as anything.

You also drove it with an unseen lubrication system that relied mostly on sheer luck. A pump in the sump sprayed oil vaguely in the path of the spinning extremities of the crankshaft, everything sloshing about to such a degree that some of the oil got into the bearings. It might have been gloriously inefficient, but it worked and crankshaft trouble was relatively rare. Early models were also amusing in retrospect because they had an oil pressure warning device on the dashboard with a diaphragm alleged to have been made from the entrails of a pig. Whether it was, or not, it was certainly prone to rot, and to drip oil with perverse regularity on the passenger's legs. Such failings were treated with the greatest amusement by owners thankful that the car kept going despite such failings. It brought a new meaning to the phrase cheap and cheerful.

The crankshaft diameter was increased in 1930 and it received a central bearing in 1936, but the main bearings still grumbled and the early three-bearing cranks proved less reliable than the old ones: all part of the legend of the Austin Seven. With other modifications, the ultimate production engines increased top speed from around 40 mph to 55 mph.

The clutch also fell into the thoroughly eccentric class, which was acceptable only if you had never used anything else. Its pedal travelled only about a quarter of an inch from fully disengaged to very engaged. Leaping kangaroos probably perfected their technique after watching the antics of Austin Sevens sold in Australia. Until 1930, the car had only three gears, engaged by a floppy lever (which, like everything else about the Seven, you soon got used to using). It did not receive the four-speed gearbox it really needed until 1932, and even then the ratios were odd, to say the least. One thing was certain, keen drivers could always rely on finding themselves in the wrong gear, but for people who were content to tootle along, it didn't matter.

Changing down to descend hills was every bit as important as changing down to climb them. It was true that few cars had four-wheel brakes like the Austin Seven in 1922, but even then most of them were better at stopping with rear brakes only. This was because the Seven's system was simply the cheapest way to comply with the law that all cars had to have two independent forms of braking. The back ones were worked by a foot pedal, with drums so small and inefficient that they didn't do much good, and the front ones, operated by hand, were even worse. This was partly because the front brake cables pulled in a diagonal line, rather than a straight one, and tended to bend the brake levers outwards rather than pull them back into action. And the front brakes, which should have been more powerful for an ideal balance, were just the opposite because of the way the axle twisted when they were applied. Herbert Austin countered criticism by asserting that good brakes encouraged bad driving; but they had to be changed, and a succession of improvements led to rod brakes for the last 1,000 or so cars, which weren't too bad.

A bewildering array of bodies were built on the Austin Seven chassis, besides the original tourer. These included sports models as a result of racing activities, vans, fixed-head coupés and saloons by 1926, with the Morris Minor as a bitter rival by 1928. Production expanded to France, Germany, Australia and eventually to the United States, with Japanese copies. David and Goliath acts in competition provided important publicity for sales, culminating in the supercharged Ulster model (recalling exploits in Britain's oldest road race, the

Sports models were soon produced on the Austin Seven's agile chassis, beginning with this delightful 'standard' model in 1924.

The works built numerous experimental competition cars – including this model in 1929 which retained the cut-outs for tourer-type rear wings.

The Seven was the car which saved the great Austin works at Longbridge. The 100,000th produced is pictured leaving the dispatch area in 1929.

The Swallow Coachbuilding Company—later to become famous for Jaguar cars—was one of the most successful builders of special bodies on Austin Seven chassis. They were made in a former munitions factory in Coventry, with grooves for the rails which carried heavy armament trucks still visible in the floor.

Tourist Trophy, held in Northern Ireland). Exotic twin cam racers emerged in the 1930s and Austin Sevens even raced at Le Mans. At the same time, a team of Grasshoppers—a particularly apt, tongue-in-the cheek, name resulting from the way they handled—contested the major trials, equivalent to today's top-line rallies.

Sir Herbert, as he became, resisted modernisation of his money-spinner for as long as possible, but eventually, in 1934, the exposed radiator all but disappeared and the bodywork distinguished the new Austin Sevens as cars of the 1930s. With strong competition from bigger Fords in the same price range, the Seven saloons waxed greater until eventually the Seven was replaced in 1939 by the Austin Eight.

By that time, more than a quarter of a million people had bought new Austin Sevens and they continued to be a common sight in Britain until the late 1950s when the introduction of a safety test for cars more than ten years old dramatically reduced their numbers. In the meantime, a whole new sub-culture had built up, converting these ultra-light cars into competition machines, such

Open-topped tourers continued to be popular throughout the Austin Seven's production life despite the success of the saloon. This is a 1934 Opal two-seater which sold for only £100 and found just enough room for a third person!

notable designers and drivers as Colin Chapman, of Lotus fame, cutting their teeth on Austin Seven specials.

By the 1960s, the Austin Seven, long a national pet, was being enthusiastically preserved as one of the few vintage cars you could, quite practically, drive every day. Restoration was helped by the fact that they were so small that they were easy to handle. The Austin Seven's diminutive size was also its strength in that it didn't take up much room, and often survived in the backs of garages, in barns and places like that, where bigger cars might have been cast out to the scrapman because they took up too much room.

Because of this sustained level of interest, the sporting aspects, and the very hardiness of these cars, there have always been sufficient Austin Sevens in existence to support an active spares industry, with the result that it is still practical to rebuild a car from many diverse pieces; even to use it every day like many of the enthusiasts I met while writing this book.

The Austin Seven eventually grew up to become the Ruby in 1934 with such refinements as bumpers, trafficators that swung back into the door jamb, and even a cowled radiator.

II

The Early Austin Sevens

Although the first Austin Sevens were conceived and built in a matter of months, it would be ten full years before they changed radically—and even then their character was much the same. Herbert Austin began to think seriously about the Seven as we know it only when dramatic changes in Britain's car taxation laws sent the cost of licencing soaring. From 1 January 1921, it cost £23 a year to tax the Austin 20, one of his versions of the Model T Ford, instead of £6. Austin countered this alarming rise with a stopgap model, a scaled-down 20 called the 12, but he could not sell enough to overcome such a sudden and ferocious rise in tax. Plans for a very small car that had lain dormant in his sketchbook for at least a year were suddenly resurrected as a matter of the utmost urgency.

Tax on the rival Bullnose Morris had gone up from £3 a year to £12—about a month's wages for the average middle-class buyer—so anything that could be saved from even that smaller sum was of paramount importance. The tax was based partly on a formula involving engine size, so initial thoughts fixed on an air-cooled twin-cylinder engine of the type used in Jowett and Rover light cars, in order to bring the tax down to £8.

At that time, a motor manufacturers' year normally ended with their factory's summer holidays, beginning afresh when the staff returned. August was the operative date for Austin, so late in that month in 1921, design work began in earnest on the new car. A bright young draughtsman, Stanley Edge, was seconded to help Austin at his boss's home near the factory at Longbridge, Birmingham. Edge was nearly 18, but had already worked at Longbridge since he was 14, the normal school-leaving age then. He was probably picked for such an honour because he had plenty of free time and did not mind working eccentric hours; his colleagues were, almost without exception, mature men with family commitments and the only time that Austin had free with any regularity was in the evening. Edge was also an unusually studious young person and seized his opportunity. And so a man and a boy nearly forty years his junior (the age of majority was twenty-one in those days), set about designing a car which would save them both, and thousands of others at Longbridge and their suppliers. Fortunately they got along very well and Edge was able to offer a feasible alternative to, first the noisy and frequently rough-running, air-cooled twins used by Jowett and Rover, and then, the next step up, a three-cylinder radial—taking its inspiration from the fighter planes which had captured everybody's imagination in the 1914–18 war.

One of Edge's tasks was to produce a list of contemporary small cars and their salient dimensions. It would appear that the Peugeot Quadrilette, introduced in April 1921, emerged from this source as an outstandingly attractive example of just what Austin wanted. Its similarity to the eventual Seven was far too marked for it not to have been a considerable influence.

The Baby Peugeot's most notable feature was that it had the world's smallest four-cylinder engine, which was also water-cooled. This meant that it was far smoother to operate than the less well-balanced twins, and much quieter, because its water jackets absorbed more of the noise of detonation within the cylinders. So much for sophistication: if Peugeot could make such a unit work, Austin was sure that he could do it better. He seems to have taken little persuasion by Edge once he had worked the twins and radial three engines out of his system.

Once the decision had been taken early in 1922 to build a small water-cooled four, Edge set about calculating the exact dimensions. It was a task he enjoyed because he was a keen student of engine design and Austin was too busy for such details; he preferred to inspect the finished job and decide whether it looked right. Eventually Edge opted for a bore and stroke of 55 mm × 77 mm to give a capacity of 696 cc, slightly more than the Peugeot's 668 cc, achieved with a 50 mm × 85 mm bore and stroke. Exactly why he settled on these dimensions— $2\frac{1}{8}$ ins × 3 ins by contemporary English measures—has not been revealed, but

The Austin Seven engine pictured is one of the earliest produced, in 1924, with its dynamo at the front, magneto low at the side alongside the crankcase, and starter motor mounted above the flywheel behind the engine.

Edge had to work within the confines of what Austin could produce economically. As a result, the engines followed their normal practice of having an aluminium crankcase and cast-iron cylinder block—a good deal more convenient than that of the Peugeot, which laboured on with an old-fashioned integral head.

There was a marked similarity to other features of the French car's engine, however. The crankcase was very much the same with a roller bearing at either end, supplemented in the case of the British car by a ball race at the front to take thrust and to form an extra support for an extension of the crankcase nose which would carry the timing gears. The use of white metal main bearings would have made the engine longer, which Edge and Austin, quite rightly, considered an undesirable feature in a car of minimum size. But white metal, conventional at the time, was used for the big end bearings. They were lubricated through drillings in the crankshaft web, the mist of oil slopping about to such an extent that it served to lubricate the roller bearings adequately as well. On the whole, this was the cheapest way of keeping the bottom end well oiled, avoiding the necessity of using lots of pipes.

The inlet and exhaust valves, all eight of them, were lined up along the right-hand side of the cylinder block when viewed from the front, and were operated by a low-mounted camshaft. This was driven from the timing gears at the front of the crankcase with tappets operating the valves. The camshaft drive also operated a horizontally-mounted magneto for the ignition. A starting handle that occupied a permanent spot in front of the radiator was used to engage the crankshaft and swing everything into action.

The valves were strung along the nearside side of the engine like a washing line, as can be seen in this sectioned example.

In reality, the cylinder head was an adaptation of one pioneered—and patented—by Sir Harry Ricardo in 1921. It was in this area of technical development that Edge felt at his strongest. The cylinder heads of the bigger Austins had compression ratios of no more than 4.75:1 because their designers felt that this was the most that a touring car could stand. Edge had different ideas, having seen far higher ratios used in competition without damage. His eventual design hovered around 5.6:1 and worked very well to give a relatively vigorous output.

Ricardo's theories in relation to combustion chamber shape helped here and combined conveniently with the general lay-out of Edge's engine. Everything hinged on the need to keep the engine short, and maximum advantage was taken of the lack of a central main bearing. The result was a block only 11 ins long and 5 ins wide but with the 'washing line' of valves along one side and the need for central water holes, the combustion chamber shape was almost fixed in advance; it was perhaps lucky that it was an advanced shape for the time that would be exceptionally responsive to tuning. An exact copy of Ricardo's sparking plug placement was found to be advantageous.

If engine design was Edge's strong point, he had not yet had time to learn much else to the same degree. He was well able to calculate the gear ratios needed, clutch diameter, and so on, but he relied on Austin's guidance as to exactly how the other mechanical items should be made. Where possible, the Peugeot's example appears to have been followed, with a triangulated chassis frame terminating in the quarter elliptic rear springs, and a Model A Ford-style

The rear end of the chassis, with its quarter elliptic springs, followed the example set by Peugeot.

The front of the chassis used a transverse leaf spring, anchored at the centre in the manner of the Model A Ford, with the addition of a single friction-type shock absorber soon after production started.

transverse leaf spring at the front. The Peugeot also used a torque tube to locate the rear axle and radius arms at the front.

The Austin copied this basic A-shaped lay-out faithfully, with the front radius rods being located on a crossmember that also supported the back of the gearbox. In company with the engine, this unit had four solid mountings, a method which might seem incredible by today's standards where mountings of great flexibility are needed to iron out bad vibrations. But this arrangement worked well in the 1920s because the chassis frame twisted a lot, in marked contrast to the rigidity of a modern monocoque. A second crossmember united the rear ends of the sidemembers and provided a ball joint mounting for the front of the rear axle's torque tube. This was an area in which not even Austin could get away with a great deal of flexibility, especially when it came to the engine's twisting ability. In fact, one prototype with a money-saving open shaft hopped around in the most hilarious manner as the revving engine produced more torque!

The rear ends of the sidemembers—which were of steel pressed into a 'top hat' section—were boxed in to provide housings which located the five-leaf rear springs. A drilled stay between the front and rear crossmembers made a direct stress path from the front radius arms to the torque tube at the back. It stabilised the rear crossmember at the same time.

Austin was convinced that four-wheel brakes would soon become an established feature, even on the smallest of cars, and opted for the transverse leaf spring at the front as the most efficient way of saving money in production. A conventional front axle located only by half-elliptic leaf springs did not have to take the stress of braking at the time and would have had to have been beefed up a lot to cope. These forces could have been countered by radius rods, but when

A demonstration chassis, painted white, was prepared by the works in 1928 to show all the Austin Seven's salient features.

they were used it was possible to get away with employing only one spring and a relatively light axle—which is just what Austin did.

He was not at all impressed with the relative complexity of the Peugeot's gearbox, either, which was in a unit with its rear axle. Austin insisted on his Seven being fitted with a three-speed 'crash' gearbox in a conventional position,

The Austin Seven's three-speed crash gearbox was of conventional and durable design.

with an open shaft leading to the second shaft enclosed in the torque tube. The rear axle was also of conventional design, with a spiral bevel drive and three-quarter floating format. It also had a differential, which was quite normal, but made it a lot more refined than the solid-axle baby Peugeot. Edge worked out the gearing at 4.5:1, 8:1 and 14.5:1 overall with a 17:1 reverse and 26-inch × 3-inch wire wheels. Ground clearance was 9 ins—amazing by today's standards, but a necessity in the early 1920s when many roads were far less smooth than those in use today; it was also quite common then to drive your car across fields to remote cottages. The sheer flexibility of the chassis and springs allowed a great deal of wheel movement, which made the car ideal for off-road use although it was rather springy on hard surfaces.

The four-wheel brakes were an advanced feature for 1922—even if they did not work well because Austin had them made from as few parts as possible. The rear ones were operated by cables from a foot pedal, and the front by similar means from a hand lever. An experienced driver could use this system to advantage, varying the pressure between front and back, providing, of course, that it was adequate in the first place. But most drivers just slammed them on simultaneously. There were a number of deficiencies, notably in the cable geometry. One fault that manifested itself as a result was the way in which the front brakes came on at full lock as the cables shortened! But this sort of thing was all considered part of the fun in an era when all cars had quirks. Austin countered any possible criticisms by saying that normally a driver would use

The mechanical layout of the Austin Seven—this drawing is of a 1931 saloon—can be seen here in detail, with the two main-bearing engine, petrol tank mounted on the scuttle, providing a gravity feed, high-mounted radiator intended to operate on a thermo-syphon principle, sudden-death clutch, neat little gearbox, and divided propeller shaft leading to the conventional spiral-drive rear axle with differential. The brakes were operated by the cables under the chassis, with adjustment at a point near the bottom of the hand lever.

THE AUSTIN SEVEN SALOON
—— IN SECTION ——

The original Austin Seven—this one was pictured in 1922—was intended to carry the average family of man and wife, plus two children on the shelf at the back. But soon it was adapted to carry far more adventurous loads.

front and rear brakes together only when travelling in a straight line. He wouldn't be able to jerk on only the front brakes going round a corner, and cause the front wheels to skid, because his hands would be too busy steering!

Worm-and-wheel steering gear was used until 1937 with a large, 15-inch steering wheel. This sort of diameter was common for the 1920s.

The basic dimensions of the car, a 6 ft 3-inch wheelbase and a 3 ft 4-inch track, represented a size that was the smallest possible that could take two adults and, perhaps, some children sitting behind them, in a reasonable degree of comfort. The actual width of the body was the same as the track, 3 ft 4 ins, with 1 ft 8-inch wide doors, which were considered quite large at the time. The body construction—in open tourer form at first—was quite novel, and very advanced. Steel wings and floor panels were stamped out on huge presses and assembled onto the chassis, with aluminium body panels beaten out by hand, and hung on a wooden frame secured to the chassis. Austin's form of mass production, which subsequently became the norm, saved a great deal of labour but needed heavy investment in the presses and tooling needed to shape the panels. The new small

Austin's bodywork was minimal to keep down its cost, and had a curious scalloped scuttle with wings which were only slightly more expansive than those fitted to a bicycle. No running boards were used at first, but the car came with full weather equipment—hood and detachable sidescreens—that made it much more comfortable than a motor cycle combination. The Austin scored, of course, in that it cost very little more than its three-wheeled rival.

Hood up, the Chummy was a snug little machine, and far nicer than a motor-cycle combination! This picture was taken in 1922 and shows the addition of running boards for the 1923 model.

Petrol was carried in a four-gallon tank under the bonnet, mounted on the scuttle. The radiator core was exposed with water cooling working on the thermo-syphon principle to save working parts, although it had to be boosted by a fan as early as October 1923. Some cars had a cable starter like that used on an outboard marine engine, but this did not work very well and the standard handle was generally better.

There was no luggage boot as such—not many cars had them then—but there were two large lockers under the adjustable bucket seats at the front, and one under the back seat. An oil pressure warning device was fitted, but no speedometer because it wasn't a legal necessity then. An electric horn that could be worked from the dashboard occupied a place under the bonnet.

In its earliest form, the engine produced 10 bhp at 2,400 rpm, with its official RAC rating set at 7.2 bhp. Its output was quite sufficient to endow the car with a lively performance (for the day) because of its low overall weight (around 6.5 cwt), although the gearing was high for ultimate economy. At least the RAC rating's insistence on a long stroke helped overcome such tall gear ratios. Hardly more than 100 cars had been produced, however, than the engine was bored out to 2.2 ins (56 mm) with a 76-mm stroke to take fuller advantage of the RAC's rating, which then worked out at 7.8 bhp. The power output in this form was 10.5 bhp from 747.5 cc.

These changes, including improvements to the piston rings to reduce oil

As early as 1923, Austin were experimenting with radically different body styles for the Seven, including this doctor's coupé which had easy-to-clean disc wheels. Demand for the standard cars remained so high, however, that the coupé did not go into production.

As early as 1923, Austin were experimenting with radically different body styles for the Seven, including this doctor's coupé which had easy-to-clean disc wheels. Demand for the standard cars remained so high, however, that the coupé did not go into production.

consumption, were introduced at chassis number A1-101 in March 1923, with running boards as an added luxury. They were of considerable benefit in rural areas in the 1920s, such was the prevalence of puddles by the roadside!

The windscreen was also altered at the same time, being made taller with a cross tube at the top supporting a small moveable section. This arrangement offered better visibility, especially in fog, when the driver could peer through the opened slot at the top.

Meanwhile Austin's son-in-law, Captain Arthur Waite, embarked on a season's racing with a lightweight two-seater Seven prepared at the factory; modifications were few as it was intended to highlight any weaknesses in the production cars. But it had a fabric body, a higher (4.5:1) rear axle ratio, Hartford adjustable competition dampers and Pirelli racing tyres to help it attain higher speeds. At the same time, coachbuilder Gordon England, who had had some success with the marque ABC, also decided that the new Seven would make a good competition car. He managed to talk Austin into letting him take over Waite's machine after the factory had built the captain an even lighter single-seater. These cars, and two other similar prototypes, had their power outputs increased as the season went on, with twin Cox-Atmos carburettors, triple-branch exhaust manifolds and high-lift cams. In this form they were able to hold 5,000 rpm for reasonably long periods—until their rear big end bearings, which were furthest from the source of lubrication, became starved. Austin got round this problem, which had not manifested itself at lower revs, by designing tubes that could be attached to the crankshaft using its centrifugal force to give a freer flow to the vital bearing. These tubes were then fitted to production engines—justifying his policy, at the time, of improving the breed by racing

Capt. Waite's 1923 racer is pictured with him behind the wheel after winning the Easter Small Car handicap at Brooklands.

The 1923 Austin Seven featured detail improvements such as a windscreen with a hinged top section for better visibility in fog, and running boards as standard. But the front shock absorber had not yet arrived...

substantially standard cars rather than ones which bore little resemblance to the everyday product.

Such matters were of less concern to Gordon England and he developed his cars' engines to a far greater degree, with lightweight pistons, better valves and springs, a higher-compression cylinder head, and forced feed lubrication.

These machines were very successful in competition and led to the introduction of two new models in January 1924, the Sports and the Brooklands Super-Sports. The Sports models were little different from standard except that they had a rakish two-seater body necessitating a re-angled steering column and a longer gearlever. Their ignition was advanced to give a little extra power at the expense of smoother running, and they were quicker than the normal tourer as a result. They also had the luxury of an electric starter as standard, shock absorbers front and rear, and a speedometer. The top of their windscreen was detachable for high-speed driving in the region of 50 mph—very zippy!

This sports model, built in 1925, had full weather equipment—if you did not count sidescreens as being necessary—although of a rather strange shape.

The Brooklands Super-Sports machines were quite different, with stream-lined aluminium bodies and far more powerful engines like that in Gordon England's racer. In essence, they were production versions of the previous year's competition two-seater and cost nearly half as much again as a tourer by the time you had added wings, hood and windscreen for use on the road. But they received a lot of publicity from certificates confirming that they had achieved 75 mph on test at Brooklands.

In more mundane circles, a delivery van body that could carry 2.5 cwt was listed for the tourer chassis from October 1923 as the more expensive models' extras—such as the mechanical or more expensive electrical starter—were offered as options. Soon after, their smoother fabric front joint to the propeller shaft, speedometer, and shock absorbers were phased in between February and May 1924.

The early customers proved as adept as the racing men when it came to developing the Seven, but more by just adjusting the weight and by ignorance than anything scientific. The popular conception was often that the new Seven could carry as much as you could squeeze in rather than a set weight. Within weeks of the car's introduction it became common to see four adults and piles of shopping almost overflowing the edges of the body; I can well remember a relative using his early Seven to cart a huge white pig to market that seemed to weigh almost as much as the car and had to be roped into both front and rear seats!

This sort of overloading caused the body to crack around the door apertures because it received no support from a chassis aft of the rear spring mountings. Complaints on this score were countered by providing pressed steel extensions to the chassis that could be secured by the same clips that held the springs. Then people complained that the door latches stopped them slamming the doors when their hands were full. So spring latches were substituted, which meant that the doors no longer stopped their openings from flexing and before long there were further complaints about cracking. The spring latches were also a retrograde step in that you could now fall out of an Austin Seven quite easily!

But other changes were definitely steps in the right direction. Starting from cold proved difficult on some early cars and was much improved when a different make of magneto was fitted to give a better spark at low revs. The valve stems were also modified for the same reason and the mechanical starter, listed as an option from May 1922, was soon superceded by the far more convenient electric starter. This needed a heavier-capacity battery and larger dynamo, however, and they were fitted by the end of 1924.

The piston ring specification was changed to cut oil consumption, and so was the oil gauge, which was fitted to a few cars and had been upsetting some people. They had been tricked into thinking that there was something seriously wrong with the lubrication system because they could see the pressure dropping dramatically as the engine warmed up. These gauges also tended to leak badly, so they were replaced by a black button which popped out when the oil pump was working; it retracted into its bezel a little when the oil became thinner, but fewer people were alarmed because its movement was less graphic. It was unfortunate, though, that it did not give the same eye-catching warning as the earlier gauge when there really was something amiss, such as a blocked jet. This would cause the gauge's needle to jerk round sharply. In such an event, you had to stop immediately, remove a plug above the offending jet, and poke it clear with a piece of wire. Otherwise you could soon ruin a bearing or seize a piston!

Transmission trouble was quite common on the early cars as well, partly because of the difficult clutch and partly because of the lack of shock absorbers. Spectacular kangaroo-style starts, particularly by novices struggling to get the hang of the sudden-death clutch, were made worse by the total lack of damping for the rear axle. The car leaped around in the most vigorous manner, with the transmission taking nearly all the strain. It is significant that transmission trouble decreased significantly when shock absorbers came along, although Longbridge also changed the angle of the final drive teeth to lessen the torque loading. The rear hubs were fitted with greasing points to improve lubrication and the ball race seatings were modified to combat splitting.

Delusions of grandeur on the race track caused many adventurous owners to over-tighten their optional Hartford shock absorbers, resulting in the mounting brackets breaking. This was only alleviated when Austin replaced the shock absorbers with their own standard fittings, which could not be adjusted easily, in June 1925. Enthusiastic drivers were also prone to advance the ignition too far in the hope of extracting a lot of extra power. But this practice resulted only in very rough running, which in extreme cases, could make the flywheel vibrate so much that the clutch slipped! A stop for the clutch pedal was eventually cast into the bellhousing after heavy-footed drivers had sheared the taper pins which secured the declutching levers.

The standard body, the third car style for the Seven to be produced by the factory, then adopted a C designation in good time for the 1925 season. The overall aim was to provide more space. In pursuit of this ideal, the doors were widened, with sloping rear edges to ease access to the rear shelf. The scuttle was cleaned up with flush sides, and the bonnet modified accordingly. The windscreen was mounted vertically and more space—rather than just the illusion of it—was created in the back. This factor was accentuated by raising the back of the hood so that there was more headroom. The original safe-and-sound door catches re-appeared.

The dashboard was also tidied up with the by-now standard speedometer flanked by the oil indicator button, magneto switch, dimmer, horn push, air strangler and switch panel. By this time (June 1924), flanges to exclude mud had already been incorporated in the brake drums.

Numerous coachbuilders began offering special bodies on Austin Seven chassis—particularly of a sporting nature—and keen pricing of standard cars helped keep demand far in excess of supply.

The next major changes was in March 1925 when 'balloon' tyres were fitted. The earlier high-pressure beaded-edge rubberware, which when combined with quite stiff springing (particularly when shock absorbers were fitted) made the ride less than comfortable on rough surfaces. The Americans had got over this problem with low-pressure tyres on rims which had wells to prevent the tyre rolling off; so Dunlop took up this idea with a 26 × 3.50-inch wired-edge tyre for the Seven.

Meanwhile Waite had been experimenting successfully with supercharging for competition work although it would be some time before this advanced form of tuning would be seen on standard cars because of the great expense involved. Gordon England, for one, was against it because it would raise the price of a racing Seven to a staggering £800, so much extra work was needed on the engine. At that price, he saw only a small market, and concentrated on other forms of development, such as a Cup model that was cheaper than the Super-Sports. This variant, introduced in August 1925, had a fabric two-seater body with a domed back, which became a predecessor to the first saloon body to be fitted to an Austin Seven, in May 1926.

This body was an adaptation of the Weymann fabric bodies that had been developed from aeroplane practice, where strong water-resistant cloth was stretched over a wooden frame. The result was very light and reasonably durable. England's version was even better because it had a complete plywood shell to support the fabric rather than just the bones of one. Its weight was still low, so it was made a little longer—2 inches—than the tourer, so that it was less cramped. The doors were as wide as possible, with sliding windows, and the entire tent-like structure mounted on the chassis at three points—one on either side near the door pillars and one in the middle at the back. These mountings employed Hardy fabric discs that enabled the chassis to flex extensively inside the body without disturbing it unduly. The instrument panel was mounted rigidly on the chassis to avoid complication and the headlamps, formerly on either side of the scuttle, moved forward to what had become a more conventional position either side of the radiator surround. Small sidelights were fitted to the wings. The windscreen did not open and was provided with a suction-operated wiper.

In the meantime, further development was going ahead at Longbridge on the standard tourer that resulted in its body being made wider and longer with more kneeroom for a D designation in February 1926. The windscreen was curved around the scuttle and the hood frame revised so that it could be folded without taking down the sidescreens. The door fastenings were changed yet again in an attempt to give the best of both worlds—the slamming and the security—with spring catches and handles so that they could be opened from outside when the sidescreens were in position.

Despite these improvements in the tourer's body, demand increased greatly for the relatively weatherproof new saloon that was being assembled alongside

The scuttle was cleaned up, with flat, rather than scalloped, sides in 1925 and the doors widened, with sloping rear edges to make access easier. The back of the hood was also raised so that there was more room, and soon after 'balloon' tyres were fitted. Then, for 1926, when this model was produced, the windscreen was curved around the scuttle and the hood frame revised so that the car could be run with the hood down and the sidescreens up. Note also the neat revised door handles.

The first metal-bodied Austin Seven saloon was introduced in 1926 with sliding windows and rear-hinged doors in contrast to those of the open tourer.

the tourers at Longbridge—and Austin introduced a metal version in 1926. The Gordon England method of construction was too time consuming on a large scale, although it remained as an upmarket option that appealed to a number of people because of its lightness. A metal van version was introduced at the same time as Longbridge's saloon and towards the end of 1926 the headlamps of all Sevens were moved forward to the Gordon England position. But sidelamps were considered to be a waste of money and the headlamps were returned to the scuttle in January 1927 when police objected that they did not provide a good indication of the car's width. Other changes made during this period included a horn switch in September 1925, revised wheel rims in March 1926 and deeper frame sidemembers in conjunction with stronger rear springs soon after the

Fabric-bodied saloons, such as those built by Gordon England, continued to be popular for a while because they were lighter than the steel cars.

This left-hand-drive open Seven produced under licence in Germany was the Dixi and became the fore-runner of today's BMW cars. The car pictured is a 1930 model.

heavier metal saloon and van bodies were phased in. Larger brake drums were introduced from September 1926, and a more convenient four-piece bonnet, screenwiper and Lucas switchboard by October.

For a variety of reasons, Austin had few rivals in this field initially, and as a result the specification of standard cars changed little during 1927. Demand for something different was well met by numerous special bodies, and a certain amount of tuning, by specialists; a deal was done for the Seven to be produced in Germany as the Dixi, followed by another for it to appear as the Rosengart in France. Detail improvements carried out included a spring fitting for the petrol filler cap, a longer, cranked, gearlever to save the driver from having to lean forward, and reshaped gear teeth for a better mesh. There was also a good deal

The French Rosengart model—seen leading a group of Austin Sevens during the 1984 Festival of Yesteryear at Brands Hatch—was also quite successful for a while.

of fiddling about with the speedometer. The original belt-driven instrument was discontinued, the drive now being taken from the gearbox (in September 1927). And then, only a month later, the gearbox casing was modified for a revised drive and a new third motion shaft.

Triumph brought out a new Super Seven at the same time, but were not seen to present much of a threat because the price was ten per cent higher. Then the bombshell dropped. Morris, Britain's biggest motor manufacturer at the time, introduced the Minor, in May 1928, as a direct rival to the Seven, and with a more advanced overhead camshaft engine. The most immediate result was a

Although outwardly similar to earlier models, the 1928 Austin Seven tourer featured many improvements to help counter the menace of the new Morris Minor.

Radiator muffs have always been popular wear on Austin Sevens, particularly in winter!

price-cutting war and wholesale small improvements that had been held up in the pipeline.

Outwardly, the radiator drain tap of the Seven was moved to a more convenient position. But out of sight, the frame's side members were extended at last to give better body support. The rear shock absorber mountings were simplified at the same time and the dampers themselves improved with brass rubbing discs at their friction points; rubber bushing replaced wood in the axle arm anchorages. The brake drums were also secured by three screws to keep them in place while a wheel was being changed. The clutch was modified with a longer splined first motion shaft and wheel spokes were beefed up. Other improvements were introduced in haphazard form as and when they could be fitted in on the production line: starting handles were extended, for instance, to clear the radiator muffs which had become popular for winter. But this change took place in April 1928, as soon as that winter was over!

Other needs, such as styling, were more pressing. A new, taller, radiator was fitted in time for the 1929 season with a nickel-plated surround to make the Seven look more impressive. Inside the car, the speedometer moved to the centre of the instrument panel so that two useful cubby holes could be let in each side. The steering column was modified to accept a more modern flat steering wheel instead of the old dished type and the headlamps were moved back to their place alongside the radiator. Two separate bulbs were fitted inside each enlarged casing to meet legal requirements. The interior of saloons was much improved by fitting a less-claustrophobic single-piece

The doors were made much wider on the 1929-model saloon, sporting its new high scuttle line, one-piece windscreen and nickel-plated radiator.

windscreen and scuttle ventilators, while tourers had to put up with door handles that pointed downwards—probably for reasons of safety. The popularity of special bodies also led to the introduction of a factory coupé, with a body made of metal except for the top, which was in fabric. In August 1928, the Seven's radiator cowl was made taller and more impressive, with nickle plating; the wings were also subtly refashioned. And in the next month bodies with wider doors where phased in, to meet a London Motor Show deadline, although the changeover was not completed until December.

Of more recent interest, coil ignition, which has now become universal, was phased in at the same time to give smoother low-speed running, although it was more sensitive to the use of the advance and retard control.

Attempts were made to alleviate a tendency for the engine to over-oil itself. New pistons, with three, instead of two, compression rings were fitted from January 1929—but they only made matters worse, so the older pistons with an oil ring in place of the third compression ring, were returned in August that year. In October 1929, the diameter of all the crankshaft bearings except the front one, was increased and the webs beefed up to make the bottom end stronger.

The tourer, however, retained the earlier body style with narrow doors so that the sidescreens could be adequately supported.

The supercharged sports model built from 1928 had a lowered chassis and sturdy open two-seater body, the spare wheel being concealed under a lid in the tail. The rear number plate was normally carried across the top of the tail.

New connecting rods, bolts and pegs, new rear bearing housings and bolts and a shorter oil jet were needed to clear the new crank. The flywheel was also modified to accept a wider taper at the end of the crankshaft and the old oil seal that tended to leak was replaced with an oil return thread machined into the bearing cover. This feature was also adopted on the first and third motion shafts in the gearbox, which was converted to a ball change from chassis number 99,001, still in October.

Other notable modifications in the earlier part of 1929 included a cheaper die cast FZB carburettor and a redesigned rear axle and torque tube in May.

By 1930, when this engine and gear-box were pictured, the casting had been simplified and coil ignition adopted.

Servicing was made much easier with the new rear axle because the torque tube was now screwed in rather than retained by a flange.

But the chief change was to the body. It was revised not only to make it look different—and then, hopefully, give the impression that Austin were marketing a new car—but was enlarged at the same time to compete more realistically with the Morris Minor, which could carry four adults in reasonable comfort. An invaluable extra three inches were liberated in the Seven's rear passenger area and the roofline was bowed upwards to give more headroom. The scuttle was redesigned to accept a new, higher, bonnet line—which not only made the car look more powerful in many people's eyes, but enabled the petrol tank to be resited in a more convenient position. Austin had begun to make their own radiators by the time the new, E-designation, body was adopted in September, and the deeper surround was chromium-plated for maximum sales appeal.

The headlamps returned to the new radiator's sides, with legal necessities being met by inserting two bulbs in enlarged casings. The wings were resculptured and fitted with new supporting stays. Detail refinements made a world of difference inside: rain guttering was provided on the interior of the tourer's windscreen to safeguard the occupants' ankles, and a scuttle ventilator was provided at last. Saloon bodies received a less claustrophobic single-piece windscreen. Spring clips for the hood stays on the tourer proved a lot less fiddly and cost less to make than the old straps. The speedometer was repositioned so that long cubby holes could be let in each side of the instrument panel and doors were fitted with handles inside.

The extra carrying capacity of the Seven influenced a lot of things. The front springs were made more flexible to help keep the wheels on the ground when there was a lot of weight in the back. This meant using eight thinner leaves in place of five heavier ones. The rear springs and many of the back axle

The standard Seven saloon remained as Austin's best seller, this model being photographed in 1930.

There were numerous variants on the standard theme, including this 1930-model sliding roof saloon.

components were strengthened and a longitudinal strut braced the chassis. The brakes were coupled at last so that all four could be worked by the foot pedal and the handbrake was fitted with a trigger mechanism to make it easier to operate.

This system had been used effectively in the Ulster sports models that went into production in 1929, although braking ability was never high in the order of Austin priorities. Neither was good roadholding, although attempts to improve handling were made on the Ulster providing not too many standard components had to be changed. The car's centre of gravity was lowered by fitting a dropped front axle beam and reverse camber spring, which was bound in cord, racing style, to make it stiffer. This lowered the front 2.5 ins and the chassis by 3 ins, the rake of the rear springs being modified in accord. A longer torque member had to be fitted and the angle of the steering column was changed. Modifications

to increase the power of the engine were more far-reaching, so the clutch was uprated with double springs and cast iron liners.

One of the most important aspects of the changes to the engine was the adoption of pressure-fed lubrication through the nose of the crankshaft—by way of a leather gland that had only a limited life (but, then, the Ulster was meant to be a competition car, and a higher level of maintenance was only to be expected). The connecting rods were machined all over to make them stronger and a more aggressive camshaft profile used, valve lift being increased by one third. These longer, tulip-shaped, valves were made from higher-quality steel and were fitted with double springs like the clutch. This Ulster engine became available in both blown and unblown form.

The supercharger used was a vane-type Cozette, made in France with a carburettor to match. It was driven by a train of gears to its position on the near side of the cylinder block, which was modified to withstand the boost. Ten 0.375-inch studs were used to secure it to the crankcase in place of the normal eight 1.3125-inch studs. The crankshaft was also increased in diameter on blown engines from 1.1875 ins to 1.5 ins to make the bottom end stronger. But whether the engine was supercharged or not, it was fitted with a special three-branch exhaust manifold and external piping. Unblown engines had a single 30-mm updraft Solex carburettor like that used on the later Gordon England Brooklands Super-Sports models—and amazingly the price was kept down to £185 for the unsupercharged car and £225 for the blown Ulster. This was made possible by using so many standard components and producing the special parts in reasonably large quantities—but it was a far cry from the £800 estimate for a blown car only a year or so earlier.

Ulsters could be used on the road, but were really meant for competition to keep Austin's name to the fore in small car events. They had relatively roomy 3-ft wide aluminium bodies, but still needed cockpit cutaways because they did not have doors. This made the bodies stronger, lighter and simpler than many other sporting versions. Luggage room consisted chiefly of a compartment in the tail for the spare wheel, and the windscreen folded flat in the true 1920s racing tradition. In unblown form, the engine produced 24 bhp and in supercharged form, 33, within the same overall rev limit of 5,000. Gear ratios of 4.9, 7 and 12.5 with 3.90 × 19-inch wheels gave it around the same performance as the Brooklands Super-Sports. These cars were built in limited numbers until 1931, when depression swept Britain ... and the Seven really began to grow up.

Sporting types who couldn't quite run to an Ulster could still buy a neat open sports two-seater from Austin in 1930.

A fixed-head coupé was also built along the same lines as the standard sports Seven in 1930.

III
The Seven Grows Up

The introduction of a utility two-seater Morris Minor at only £100 for 1931 would have seemed like a tremendous challenge to anybody other than Sir Herbert Austin. But he did not panic and try to produce a Seven at such a low price; studies had shown that somewhere around £110 was his minimum for a metal-bodied car, and he was convinced that 'rag'—or fabric—bodies like that used in the cheap Morris were on their way out. He decided, instead, to meet the challenge with a better Seven that could be described without reservation as a full four-seater. The price of a de luxe version would be only £128, with the cost of existing, more mundane, models held at £118. In the event, when the ranges met head-on, his two-seater did not stand much chance against the cheap Morris, but the saloons held their ground well, and sales soared as soon as the de luxe version was introduced in October 1931.

The new de luxe saloon introduced late in 1931 was the first full four-seater Austin Seven with its longer wheelbase.

It was far more than a saloon with extra trimmings like those produced by the specialist body builders. It was made significantly roomier inside by moving back the rear axle by six inches. The chassis rails were extended rearwards in a straight line over a wider rear axle, which now had a track of 3 ft 7 ins. This liberated another two inches across the rear seats and meant that the trailing edge of the doors could be dropped straight down to the bottom, resulting in easier access to the back. Footwells let into the floor on either side of the propeller shaft tunnel extended beneath the front seats to give more effective leg room. The front seats could now be tilted forward to further ease entry for passengers in the back. A less obvious advantage of increasing the wheelbase to 6 ft 9 ins was that the car's ride was improved, particularly for people in the back, who now sat further in front of the axle. There was nothing worse than sitting directly over a wildly bouncing, or vibrating, back axle.

Naturally, the new, larger, car weighed more—around 10.75 cwt—so the

The long-wheelbase cars continued to be made in open form with the extra length emphasised by this picture.

rear axle ratio was lowered to 5.25:1, giving overall ratios of 5.25, 9.65 and 17.1:1. A van body with a much-improved 5-cwt carrying capacity was introduced at the same time. Some small improvements had been made during the year, including a peg-type starting handle and nut, but the chief change could be seen in the use of new-pattern wings with Lucas-Graves double filament dipping headlamps operated by a switch on the steering column. A large over-centre handle also controlled the windscreen opening.

It was at this point that the Ford Motor Company finally decided that there might be money to be made from small cars, and went as far as to show a prototype in February 1932 that bore a strong resemblance to the Austin Seven de luxe saloon.

The eventual Ford 8 production saloon had departed a lot from the prototype by the time it went on sale eight months later, but it had a synchromesh gearbox which was a great step forward in the small car field. Austin's new 10-horse-power saloon was selling well as a more obvious competitor, but it was necessary to improve the Seven as well. The most dramatic change was a four-speed gearbox introduced in September 1932, with double helical teeth on the constant mesh top gear and the third gear cluster. This was hailed as a 'silent third' box for people who had been used to the fearsome grinding of the old straight-cut gears as the Seven ascended a hill; it was also known as a 'double top' box because the overall ratios were selected as 5.25, 9.05, 14.4 and 23.3:1. This made the second gear necessary only for the steepest hills normally encountered on main roads, with the bottom ratio for emergencies and off-road work—an area in which the Austin Seven was still highly popular. The clutch withdrawal mechanism was modified at the same time to make lubrication easier.

Engine efficiency was improved by a new combined inlet and exhaust manifold, heralded as a 'thermal flow' unit because it had a more effective hot spot. It took its mixture from a horizontal Zenith carburettor rather than the earlier vertical one.

Refuelling was also made a good deal more convenient by re-siting the tank at the back with an electric petrol gauge on the dashboard as a substitute for visual checks under the bonnet. The fuel supply was maintained by an AC pump driven off the camshaft now that it could no longer rely on gravity.

A four-speed gearbox was introduced in 1932, synchromesh following on second and third gears in 1933 by the time this saloon was produced as one of the last Austin Sevens with a traditional appearance.

The new gearbox was longer than the old, so the engine was moved forward an inch in the chassis, which meant fitting a new exhaust pipe. The radiator—which had a new quick-release cap—was moved at the same time, with subsequent changes to the fan spindle length and the starting handle bracket. Not surprisingly, the long wheelbase chassis—which had been introduced only on the de luxe saloon—was now made standard on the other models. The brake drums were also widened in an attempt to reduce the all-too-common fading.

The interior was modernised by repositioning the starter motor, which had projected inside, onto the offside of the engine. It relieved the 'rather mechanical' air, said a contemporary journal, *The Light Car*. The actual starting knob, which had been worked by foot, remained on the motor, however, and was now operated by a cable control on the steering column support. The instrument panel was revised with a trendy new 'moving figure' speedometer, and the ignition was given a lock and key—standard fittings nowadays—rather than just a switch, to ease the driver's mind when the car had to be left. A warning light was provided to show that the ignition was in operation, with a lamp to light the dashboard.

Sales had been falling for the two-seater, but they were revived by a new sports model, the 65 (for 65 mph), in June 1933. It was a lot lower than the standard car, with the driver's seat only 14 ins from the ground. This was achieved by lowering the chassis as a whole with the dropped front axle from the Ulster, complete with reverse-camber spring, and flat quarter elliptic rear springs anchored below the axle. These springs were the same stiff ones as fitted to the 5-cwt van. The steering column was lowered by using the Ulster box. The only other notable change to the running gear, apart from the engine, was in the use of a 5.625 rear axle ratio for better acceleration, with the close-ratio gearbox giving 5.625, 8.38, 13.33 and 21.32 overall ratios.

The 65's engine looked almost standard although it produced 23 bhp at 4,800 rpm against 12 at 2,600 for the normal item. This dramatic increase in power was obtained by modifications including a downdraught 30-mm Zenith VE1 carburettor on a new alloy inlet manifold. The cylinder block and head were cast in a new stronger, chromidium, iron with reshaped combustion chambers. They were concentrated over the valves, containing the sparking plugs in that position, rather than over the bores. In essence, this was like that of the early Ulster cars, except that a thinner gasket was used for a higher compression now that the basic material was stronger. A high lift—around a 0.375-inch—camshaft was used with double valve springs and the valves themselves had a more secure square socket hole for adjustment rather than the old screwdriver slot.

The bottom end of the engine was suitably strengthened with a 1.5-inch diameter balanced crankshaft that was machined all over. The connecting rods were finished in a similar manner, with fully-floating gudgeon pins. Lock nuts replaced split pins to hold the 0.3125-inch big end bolts secure. The sump was much larger, with an oil capacity of one gallon, and external ribs to help cooling. The crankshaft oil ways were also modified to improve lubrication. Then an

additional sports model, the 75 (for 75 mph) was introduced in April 1934. It was close to the Ulster's specification, with a pressure-fed lubrication system, although its engine could also be fitted to the 65 at extra cost.

The bodies of both models were made from aluminium with lower-than-normal radiator grilles that presented a squarer appearance as a result. The 65's lines were much simpler, however, with a tail rounded in one plane, whereas the 75 had a more ambitious pointed tail. The shape of this tail was dictated by the necessity to cover a long-distance, 12-gallon, fuel tank with quick-release filler cap. In both cases, the spare wheel was concealed behind an opening panel. The

Two-seater sales were revived in 1933 with the introduction of the 65.

An additional sports model, the 75, was produced from 1934 with a specification closer to that of the Ulster than the 65. It soon became known as the Speedy because it was so much quicker! The body's lines were similar to those of the 65 although a good deal more refined in view of the higher price. Subsequently the 65 became known affectionately as the Nippy.

doors were quite different: on the 65, they were wide and deep for maximum convenience, while on the 75 they were shallower for extra bodily strength. Fairings around the cockpit of the 75 protected the occupants when the windscreen was removed for ultimate performance—which was expected to be in demand most of the time. Both cars were fitted with cycle-type wings.

Despite all this activity on the new car front, the standard models continued to be improved. The camshaft bearings were increased in size to make them more durable, the petrol pipe unions were redesigned to combat leaking, and the bottom of the gearlever was beefed up following many years of breakages. A more sophisticated Hardy Spicer rear universal joint was fitted to the propeller shaft from June 1933. The dip and lighting switches were improved, followed by a stop light incorporated in the rear lamp in August 1933, and semaphore-style trafficators.

More minor developments included an aluminium steering box that was bolted to the chassis instead of screwed, and a sun visor and fabric cover for the spare wheel on the de luxe saloon.

But the most important change for the average driver was the introduction of synchromesh on third and fourth gears in August 1933, in company with other Austin models. This made the Seven much easier to drive, although it would be several months before van gearboxes followed suit. Synchromesh was then extended to the second ratio from July 1934 in what was to be the last of the Austin Sevens with a traditional appearance.

IV
The Latter Day Austin Sevens

Market research indicated that most potential buyers considered the Austin Seven's appearance to be old-fashioned by 1935, although there were still thousands who did not mind its most prominent point, the traditional radiator surround. Sir Herbert Austin loathed change for change's sake, but decided that the saloon's body had to be made to look more streamlined if it was to hold its place in an ever more competitive arena. The most striking feature of the new bodies that resulted was the enclosure of the radiator in a new cowling painted in the same colour as the rest of the body. This cowl was also merged into revised front wings, the bonnet was lengthened, and all projections considered unnecessary were removed. The roofline and rear end of the car were also given more sweeping lines with an exceptionally neat lid to conceal the spare wheel. A foldaway luggage rack could also be hidden behind this cover when not in use.

The Austin Seven's chassis was re-designed for 1935 to help give more room inside a new, more modern, body with a cowled radiator.

The changes did not stop there, however. The chassis was lowered five inches in front of the rear axle so that footwells were no longer needed inside the body. This meant that the handbrake and pedals had to be altered, along with the exhaust system. A fuel filler pipe and cap protruded from the driver's side of the body, but the radiator filler cap was now concealed beneath the bonnet. The battery and toolbox were also resited under the scuttle, which was given adjustable louvres to improve ventilation in the saloon. This model also had rear windows that opened outwards at the back for the same reason. The interior was made altogether less claustrophobic by the use of more slender door pillars, which gave a greater glazed area. This general improvement in lines was highlighted by neat new bumpers front and rear on some models, and trafficators concealed within the bodywork when they were not in use. These now had an automatic cancelling device on the steering column and the dipswitch was foot-operated. The lighting system was completely revised with new headlamps and an illuminated interior panel that included a magnetic speedometer.

The appeal of these new small cars was emphasised by their names: Ruby

The radiator cowling was painted in the same colour as the body with silver centre gills, but the wings were always black.

The roofline of the Ruby merged into the back of the body in a completely different way to earlier models.

The back of the Ruby carried an elegant new cover for the spare wheel.

Costs were kept down on the two-seater tourer, the Opal, by deleting the bumpers among other items—and to such an extent that the price was only £100.

Despite its low cost, the Opal was still a delightful and well-equipped model as can be seen from this example.

for the saloon (which had smaller, 17-inch wheels, and fatter, 4.00 section, tyres); Pearl for a cabriolet (with a full-length folding roof), and Opal for an old-style two-seater to hedge bets with the diehards who wanted a traditional radiator surround. The Opal's price—only £100—was expected to be attractive, too. The open bodies on the 65 and 75, which had become known as the Nippy and the Speedy, continued unchanged.

Sir Herbert Austin's previous policy of concentrating on the de luxe saloon rather than a £100 car seemed to be vindicated by the sales figures in 1935, however. More than half the production run on Austin Sevens was made up of de luxe saloons with demand so low for the cheaper car that it was redesigned along the new lines. Few people wanted the Speedy (nee 75) either, so that was discontinued. But many customers were interested in comfort and the Moseley 'Float-on-Air' pneumatic upholstery which had been used in saloons since 1930, was introduced across the range in July. The brakes were also improved marginally by new shoes and linkages, and by the end of the year the electrical system was switched to positive earthing to combat corrosion and the Nippy had cheaper steel panels.

Early next year, 1936, the Nippy's appeal was broadened by fitting a Speedy-type pressure-lubricated engine as standard with the option of a normal saloon unit at a lower price. It would not be until the end of the year, however, that the sports models—as low-volume sellers—would receive a new engine that was introduced in the rest of the range in July.

This had a central 1.75-inch white metal main bearing to stiffen up the bottom end and allow more power to be extracted at higher revs; the result being 16.5 bhp at 3,400 rpm with a 6:1 compression ratio after the cylinder head had been redesigned along the sports model lines with 14-mm sparking plugs. The clutch action was also improved at long last by fitting a Borg and Beck type flexible plate for smoother and more progressive engagement. Detail im-

The Nippy's appeal was increased in 1936 by fitting a Speedy-style pressure-lubricated engine as standard with the option of a normal saloon car unit at a lower price.

The open road tourer continued to be made in small numbers until 1936, although very few were built on the Ruby chassis.

provements that were phased in during this period included cast-iron brake drums, steel brake shoes and semi-Girling-type brake operation.

The saloon bodies were also modernised further by fitting fully panelled doors—that is with window frames as part of the main skin pressing—and wind-up rear quarter lights. The windscreen was also realigned at a less severe angle and a new waistline incorporated. The cabriolet was then further improved in January 1937 by revising the top so that the cross braces could be removed when it was fully open.

By this time it was evident that the Seven was nearing the end of its long

The Austin Seven engine got its third main bearing in 1936.

This cabriolet, built in 1937, looked almost exactly like the Ruby saloon except for its folding roof.

production run in which more than 300,000 examples had left Longbridge, such was the popularity of bigger 8-hp cars that cost little more. Sir Herbert Austin began the process of educating the public that the Seven would have to be superceded by introducing an additional model, the Big Seven, in October 1937. This had a four-door body mounted on a similar chassis with a wheelbase 6.5 ins longer. It weighed 14.75 cwt, so it needed more power—which it received from a revised engine with a bore and stroke of 56.77 mm × 88.9 mm that gave a capacity of 900 cc. This engine was rated at 7.99 horsepower and described as giving half as much power again.

In March 1938 the new four-door Seven was translated into a two-door and in addition, called the Forlite after the number of side windows—the four-door version then being called the Sixlite.

The Forlite was intended as a direct replacement for the Seven, but it was not to be as the War Department showed considerable interest in a completely new Austin Eight, which subsequently took over. Improvements over the last two years of production included a Newton Bennett clutch and a stronger rear axle, but the last Sevens were produced in July 1939—the end of an era.

The Big Seven Forlite saloon made in 1939 showed just how far the model had come since its introduction 17 years earlier.

V

Austin Sevens By Any Other Name

The Austin Seven made an ideal base for the efforts of other car builders because its rolling chassis could be bought very cheaply. It was also quite simple to make under licence so it gave rise to versions that could be built outside Britain to avoid the complications of export tariffs and so on. Another attractive feature of building under licence was that the time spent on design and development could be saved.

This is not to say that there was not a healthy export market for Austin Sevens. But it was a market that was chiefly confined to the old Empire (later to become the Commonwealth) because of well-established trading links. In other areas it might not be worth setting up a sales organisation.

The most successful examples of Austin Sevens being produced under licence were in Germany and France, however. This was because operating conditions were similar in these countries, but exports to Germany suffered a severe handicap as a result of the First World War and the French, generally, had a completely different taste to the British when it came to cars.

The German version of the Austin Seven was the slightly more popular because it had no real competitor in Eastern Europe, but the French version also sold well because it did not look like an Austin Seven. An attempt was made to produce the Austin Seven in large quantities under licence in America, but the operation was a disaster because home-produced cars offered so much more for the same price. The 26-hp Chevrolet, for instance, had five seats, six windows and six cylinders and sold at the equivalent of £100.

It is significant in retrospect that Germany's Austin Seven represented the beginnings of the BMW car firm as it is known today. Their first factory in Munich had been set up to produce aero engines in 1916 during the height of the Great War. By 1922, four years after the war, the Bayerische Motoren-Werke (BMW) was producing boats, lorries and motor cycles. The motor cycle business expanded to such a degree that it occupied the entire Munich works, and the rapidly-expanding company took over the Dixi car company at Eisenach to move into that field in 1928. The Fahrzeugfabrik Eisenach had produced, first, Wartburgs, and then Dixis, since 1898—the last of which was the 3/15PS. This was an Austin Seven built under licence in 1927 to fulfil a gap in the

Eastern European market. When BMW took over soon after production started, these cars became known as the BMW-Dixi.

There was nothing quite like the Austin Seven in Germany, so the BMW-Dixi sold well—around 6,000 in its first year. Royalties of 2 per cent per car were split equally between Sir Herbert, who had set up the original deal, and the Austin Motor Company.

Initially, these Dixis and BMW-Dixis were simply re-bodied Austin Sevens with pretty, divided, radiator grilles that were to establish the lines of today's BMW trademark.

But it was inevitable that the design would be improved along an independent path. By 1932, the Dixi had changed completely to an 800-cc model called the 3/20PS, which had a tubular chassis and all-independent suspension that owed nothing to Austin. At the height of production, the BMW-Dixis had been leaving Eisenach at the rate of 350 to 400 a month in sports, saloon and coupé forms.

The French Austin Seven, called the Rosengart, presented a similar story. Its gap in the market had been created by the elevation of the Citroen Cloverleaf when Andre Citroen discovered that he could make a larger car for almost the same money, yet make a far bigger profit on it. Lucien Rosengart spotted the opportunity left by the departing Cloverleaf and resigned as managing director of Peugeot to concentrate on producing the Austin Seven under a similar licence agreement to BMW. Time was short in both cases before somebody else got in on the act. Rosengart decided to produce the Austin Seven on the advice of his new chief engineer, Jules Saloman, who had been responsible for the small Citroen. At first, the Rosengart, made in Paris from 1928, differed very little from the Austin Seven, except in bodywork—which, like the BMW was very attractive—and the use of a larger radiator to combat boiling while climbing mountain passes. The first bodies were three-place cabriolets with two seats at the front and one transverse at the back, like the Cloverleaf (which resembled the lucky little plant in planform).

While describing the success of the Rosengart in 1930, *The Light Car* really hit the nail on the head so far as market trends were concerned. Their correspondent in Paris reported:

> 'The contrast between the mixed reception of the Rosengart on its first appearance in France and the instantly-favourable impression made by the Austin Seven in England, when it first came out, is an example of the wide difference between French and English mentality and general taste.
>
> 'The Frenchman making a casual visit to England will tell you that the average English light car looks like a hideous square box on wheels, whilst the Englishman making a casual visit to France will tell you that the average French light car looks like a cross between a submarine and a bicycle, garnished with gimp. Both have a right to their opinions.'

Once the French had got over their reservations about the Rosengart having English ancestry, they really took it to their hearts, buying nearly as many as the Germans did of Dixis. Saloons and even a supercharged sports followed before it went the way of the Cloverleaf with a six-cylinder version of the Seven's engine, a longer wheelbase and stronger half-elliptic rear springs in 1932. After the Second World War, Rosengart tried selling a large luxury car, which did not go down at all well in the prevailing economic climate. They then reverted to a side-valve four-cylinder Austin-influenced engine (in 21 bhp form) for their Ariette tourer and Artisane saloon in 1952. The opposition from Renault and Panhard was strong, however, and despite the substitution of a more modern overhead valve engine in 1954, the marque disappeared the following year. It is interesting to note, though, that these cars bore a strong resemblance to Austin's contemporary A40 sports.

The American Austin Seven was produced under licence for what was expected to be a huge market, although previous attempts there at selling small cars in quantity had failed miserably. Austin's American director, Arthur J. Brandt, was convinced they would succeed by producing a scaled-down Chevrolet-style body on a modified Austin chassis. This very difficult task was taken on by an established Detroit designer, Count Alexis de Sakhnoffsky. He was required to produce a body with the flowing lines of a typical American car (namely a Chevrolet or Ford), which would drop straight on to an Austin chassis without compromise when it came to accommodation. Its seats had to be wide enough, it had to have enough legroom and sufficient headroom to standards based on a far larger concept. It also had to be as strong as the typical American dinosaur, but weigh only a fraction of the amount because it had 7 hp as opposed to about 30 hp. Amazingly, the American Austin went a long way towards meeting these seemingly impossible ideals and it deserved a better reception if only on this score. To meet the seating requirements, only two were provided in the space normally occupied by four. There was no open body, either, because the car had to be as strong as possible. So it was produced only in coupé or saloon form. These bodies were made almost entirely from steel and mounted on an A-shaped chassis that extended right to the back of the bodyline. Up to this point, the basic construction was similar to that of the Austin Seven, but from then on it was far more advanced. A steel floor was welded in place to make the bodyshell very stiff and strong. Thus it can be seen that it was of unitary construction and about 25 years ahead of its time. All American Austins were left-hand-drive, so the engine was built to a 'mirror image' to clear the steering gear and ease problems with the pedals. In other words, everything was on the opposite side. Sturdy bumpers were fitted front and rear, stronger 8-inch brakes to cope with the extra weight, and all threads changed to the American SAE pattern from the British Whitworth.

At first, everybody tried to kid everybody else that thousands had been ordered in the vain hope that that would be the case. But figures on anticipated orders and actual sales never came anywhere near each other. Rumoured orders of 180,000 in the first year resulted in just 8,558 sales and that was before demand fell off! The firm went into receivership in 1932 and 1934 and produced no cars in 1935 or 1936. De Sakhnoffsky restyled the American

Austin in 1937 and it was renamed the Bantam, with pressure lubrication and synchromesh. By 1940, the range had been extended to include an open tourer, convertible, estate car and van, but numbered few buyers. An offshoot was the first successful Jeep produced for the U.S. Army, but it came too late to save the Bantam. They could not produce enough and Willys, then Ford, took over.

The tale was totally different in Japan, where people wanted small cars. Three gentlemen by the names of Den, Aoyama and Takeuchi began making vehicles bearing their initials, DAT, in 1912, progressing to a totally new model, the Datson (son of DAT) in 1931. The name was changed to Datsun next year to incorporate the national emblem of the rising sun, and the firm reorganised (and then called Nissan) in 1933 to produce a copy of the Austin Seven that sold under the name Datsun. The only concession to originality was a slightly different body and a worm-drive rear axle; it is not clear whether Sir Herbert or the Austin Motor Company benefited from these activities—but the Datsun sold well until the Second World War. Subsequent Datsuns were closely based on Austins and frequently built under licence before they were renamed Nissan by the company which has become one of the biggest motor manufacturers in the world.

Activities inside England were on a much-reduced scale, chiefly involving bodybuilders such as Gordon England. One of the most successful was Swallow, which began making motor cycle sidecars in 1922, soon after the first Austin Seven appeared. Despite competition from the Austin Seven and the larger Morris Bullnose, these cigar-shaped sidecars sold very well. Production was up to 100 a week by the time Swallow moved into cars in 1927. The real reason for their success was the outstanding ability of the chief stylist and driving force behind the company, William Lyons. He was convinced that he could make a good profit from attractive, fairly expensive, bodywork, providing it was on a cheap chassis to keep down the overall price. It was not surprising that he chose the Austin Seven for his first venture into cars. Like everything for which he was responsible, it was very pretty: a neat two-seater with a 'bowl' tail and a rounded nose, the actual body being made from aluminium on a wooden frame. The Seven's rolling chassis was modified only in that it had extra angle iron to support the body at the back. Outwardly, it looked completely unlike an Austin and far more exclusive, which is the reason it sold so well at half as much again as the basic model. Customers were also attracted by the interior, which had quite luxurious seats and a fully-instrumented wooden dashboard. Lyons was able to offer an outstanding package because he knew all the tricks of the trade as well as how to style a car. One of the ways in which the lines were maintained was a good example: the Seven's radiator filler was half an inch too high for the elegant Swallow cowling. This problem was solved by laying a block of wood across the offending neck and hammering the filler down into the header tank. The demon modification worked and saved the cost of a special tank.

A saloon version of the Swallow followed in 1928, which excited such demand that the firm had to move from the seaside resort of Blackpool to the Midlands where there was more skilled labour. Production was up to thirty a

Brooklands bodies were generally as light and skimpy as possible on the early Austin Sevens, notably this wood-panelled version on a 1924 chassis.

Gordon England's Cup model was much prettier than many of the early Austin Seven specials. This is a 1927 example.

day, with other chassis being used, before Lyons started to make his own cars in 1931. These were the forerunners of today's Jaguars.

Success in competition also led to a welter of special bodies on Austin Seven chassis. One of the first was a two-seater with a pointed tail built late in 1924 by Thomas Hughes and Son of Birmingham. Like so many of these bodies, it was made from aluminium because this metal was easier to form than steel, and lighter. In this case, it was left in its natural, polished, state and fitted with a racy vee-shaped windscreen. The body weighed only 1.5 cwt complete with mahogany dashboard and hood. Soon after, a London firm, Wilsons of Victoria, built a similar body with highly flared wings after a fashion that had been established in sand-racing where it was vital to keep the wheels clear of accumulations of mud. These wings which look so extraordinary today, in place of the more conventional domed style adopted by Hughes, aroused little comment in 1925. *The Light Car* merely reported:

The Austin version of a Hansom carriage was this single-passenger taxi built as a prototype in 1925 with its meter just visible in the luggage compartment beside the driver.

'The wings have been enlarged to give increased protection from mud. A door is provided on each side, and these, combined with the aluminium-covered running boards, provide easy access to the ample seating accommodation, which is upholstered in Rexine. The rear squab is hinged to fold forward, so that the spare wheel, tools, and luggage may be stored in the tail.

'A feature of the Burghley design is the hinged three-piece bonnet, which is very convenient when engine adjustments are being carried out. The lines of the scuttle blend well with those of the bonnet.

'Two types of windscreen are available to choice—either a fixed single panel, with a slight backward slope, or a metal-framed vee type. It is probable that with the hood erected better weather protection is provided by the single-panel screen, but the vee type has a more sporting appearance, to which some owners are willing to sacrifice a degree of comfort.

'The rear of the body is decked over with polished stain walnut planking, secured with copper nails, whilst a wide aluminium beading

The doctor's coupé was not thought to have escaped from Longbridge— but one turned up at Rhayader, Wales, in July 1968!

round the top of the body does much to enhance its appearance. Ewart polished aluminium discs are fitted to the wheels.'

Nevertheless, the Burghley still looked like an Austin Seven and sold for more than the Swallow to come.

When H. Taylor and Co. of West London built a two-seater sporting body

A typical example of the Swallow bodywork which was successful on Austin Seven chassis—in this case a 1930 model.

Despite its registration number suggesting that it might be an Adler, this beautiful open tourer is in fact an American Austin Seven built in 1930.

The better-known American Bantam was a saloon that followed Chevrolet practice as far as possible. This is a 1934 model.

Numerous special Austin Sevens were built for military use, including these Scout cars pictured in 1930, two of which were fitted with huge radio aerials.

The Birmingham coachbuilding firm of Mulliners were responsible for many military Austin Sevens, including this 1930 gun carriage.

The Mulliner gun carriage built in 1932 followed the same lines as earlier models except that it had items such as the contemporary bonnet.

on the Seven chassis in 1927 they provided natty little scuttle ventilators modelled along the lines of those on a ship: Lyons promptly followed up with larger ones on the Swallow! The Taylor, which was of a similar appearance to the Nippy to come, featured pneumatic upholstery on the floor to keep down the centre of gravity. Like the Burghley, it had a vee-shaped screen, but a far snugger hood. The running boards were covered in linoleum and the car could be bought for £175 in any colour providing the chassis and wheels remained in their standard black. For the same price, the Swallow offered its distinctive rounded cowling, two ashtrays and Yale locks on the doors. Cole and Shuttleworth of West London built a rival sporting body and another by Jarvis, of Wimbledon—who were to enjoy a lot of success with M.G.s—cost £2 more. Duple, the North London bus builders, produced a sports body in steel and a tourer which could be converted into a delivery van with flexible sides! Mulliners of Birmingham and Granville Motors from London managed fabric bodies—all in the same £175 price bracket, while a Manchester firm, Arc, made a rather weird drop-head 'coupette'. Swallow offered their coupé with a detachable hard top, and one firm, Avon, at Warwick, managed to get the price of their sports Austin down to £152. The only trouble was that it looked too much like the standard tourer, which cost far less.

Taylor and Avon countered for 1929 by offering a third dickey seat for an extra £10 before Avon went on to produce their Swan sportsman's coupé, which was, in reality, an ugly duckling. Its lines were no match for those of a Swallow and sales suffered even if it did cost £15 less. In any case, Lyons soon hit back with a £10 price reduction and that put paid to all that nonsense.

Other firms followed the Gordon England line by offering cars fitted with tuning equipment. The KC Special from London had a rather old-fashioned—for 1929—steel duck's tail body on three different chassis: one, the standard Seven, two a special 65 mph sports edition, and the third, a super-sports capable of a claimed 70–75 mph. The only trouble was the cost, £185–£225, and the fact that Gordon England cars went better. Lyons hit back with a sports silencer with a 2-inch tailpipe that probably made more money in the long run!

Numerous trials specials were built before the war along the lines of the works Grasshoppers, usually with the close-up driving position like this.

But there were the odd ones with the later straight-arm position!

And this Austin Seven is doing its best to look like an M.G., even sporting dummy dumb irons.

One Captain H. O'Hagan, late of the Belgian coachbuilder Vanden Plas, had a rakish coupé built on an 18-inch longer wheelbase of which some commercial success was hoped, and a Mr W.D.T. Gairdner, of Andover, Hants, hoped for a lot of commercial interest in his creation: a six-wheeled Austin Seven. *The Light Car* thought that it was full of practical advantages:

'They lie not only in the direction of a handy form of transport for goods— and one which, incidentally, sounds the death-knell of the trailer—but in the application of the idea for passenger vehicles. The outstanding advantages are better braking—all six wheels are braked—better road adhesion, greater stability—noticeably on corners—and far greater riding comfort.

'A chassis of this kind could, of course, be fitted with a very attractive caravan body, and it could be used equally well for a van body. Instead of giving the car an appearance of being at "sixes and sevens"—an appropriate description, by the way!—the extra wheels greatly improve its general outline.

'The modifications were very simply carried out, the frame of the Austin Seven being merely extended to carry the semi-elliptic spring mountings forming part of the assembly of the third pair of wheels. The rear-wheel centres are 31.25 ins apart, the tyres being oversize, namely

Light delivery vans were built on slightly modified Austin Seven chassis as early as 1923.

The pretty open-windowed body style continued as late as 1929 for vans despite the popularity of the saloon from 1926.

Austin Seven commercial chassis were adapted for all manner of uses, including this milk-churn carrier in 1930.

This Austin Seven van-based pick-up from 1932 was described as a 'small lorry!'

High hopes were entertained for six-wheel conversions on the Austin Seven chassis, although few such vehicles were made, probably because of the restrictions on power. This works-built example had a tipping body and was presumably called a 'large lorry'.

Later vans adopted a more modern
appearance, this one being a very
rare version on the 1930 short-
wheelbase chassis.

The longer wheelbase chassis, such
as these 1932 examples, were
understandably much more attractive for van conversions.

The cheap Austin Seven commercial chassis also proved attractive for
promotional work, especially when
your firm was an Aylesbury cheese
maker!

A midget driver stands next to this extraordinary Austin Seven van conversion which was built in 1937 to publicise Moreland Matches. It was outstandingly successful partly because many heavy lorries of the period had proportionately high bonnet lines.

27 ins by 4.40 ins. Incidentally, the treads show no signs of "scrubbing" and when cornering the steering did not appear to be affected in any way—even on full lock.

'By means of T-lugs brazed on the existing rear brake-operating arms the brakes on the driving wheels are coupled up to those on the trailing wheels at the rear, and a very powerful braking system results.'

The front of a Top Hat saloon was retained and a platform body fitted. Whether or not Mr Gairdner managed to sell any replicas at £125 has not been recorded.

As the Depression of the early 1930s bit deep, the Swallow still sold well to people moving down from far more expensive cars. It was popular because it looked as though it cost a lot, it felt like it, and it did not look exactly like any other Austin Seven. Motor cycle manufacturers were also feeling the pinch, so Matchless decided to try their hand at a car body with the Seven as a base. This effort turned out to be a fabric-bodied sports aimed at the £150 price range that was unusual in that it offered enough legroom for people of more than six feet in height. It had a special narrow radiator but still looked like an Austin Seven.

Various other manufacturers, such as the Arrow coachworks in West London, offered special bodies, but largely the market was taken up by the cheaper factory Nippy and Speedy in the mid-1930s. A.E. Wright tried their hand with two- and four-seaters on the long wheelbase chassis, but competition cars aside, the only other options were military models!

VI
Contemporary Road Testers' Reports

Road tests of the Austin Seven when it was new make fascinating reading, not the least because they put items like the steering and brakes into perspective. They were considered to be very good in their day! The early tests also present a clear picture of why the Austin Seven sold so well because only a relatively small percentage of the population owned a car before the Second World War, and it was necessary to describe every aspect in detail. Road tests today tend to be far more technical, assuming a higher level of background knowledge from readers with one or more generations of motoring experience behind them. The absence of a speedometer in early cars was considered a handicap only in that it was not present to help record performance figures. Such data is now obtained by far more scientific methods that do not rely upon an implicit trust in the maker's instruments. In essence, the Austin Seven road tests stuck to the simple formula of telling what it was like to own and drive one when it was new, rather than why it behaved as it did. The world's oldest motoring magazine, *The Autocar*, published one of the first tests, in July 1923. It reported:

'For liveliness and ease of handling, the little Austin Seven can give points to many of the larger cars. Being, by virtue of its small size yet large carrying capacity, a highly original conception, the car has created an interest of which we had proof in the number of questions asked by strangers during the course of a recent road trial...

'The car is relatively so small that it is liable to give a wrong impression, which actual trial on the road dispels with startling rapidity. It is most fascinating to handle, and exhibits none of those features with which interested people sometimes seek to discredit it. For example, the wheelbase is short and the track narrow, yet the little car holds the road perfectly steadily at the speeds within its range. It can be taken round corners fast in perfect safety; it does not bounce unduly over bad surfaces; its springing is, indeed, above the average for comfort. We tried the car over a particular section of exceedingly rough road with one, two and three adults on board. With the weight of only one person the springing was, as might be expected, rather lively; with two there was a marked im-

For liveliness and ease of handling, *The Autocar* gave the early Chummy full marks—this 1922 example survived long enough to return to Longbridge for restoration in the early 1950s.

Minor inconveniences in the interior of the early Austin Sevens came in for only muted criticism from *The Autocar* in 1923.

provement, and with three exceptional comfort was attained. Over ordinary roads with two persons on board the suspension was distinctly good.

'Not the least attractive feature of the Austin is its accommodation. In the first place, there is a door on each side of the body, and, the frame being low, it is possible to step straight in from the road level without using the running boards at all...

'All the seat cushions are noticeably soft and comfortable; the steering wheel comes nicely within reach, and the pedals are convenient to the feet, save that the brake and accelerator are a trifle close together. The change-speed lever, as is often the case with unit construction of engine and gear box, is rather far forward, and in order to reach it one has to lean forward in the seat. The gear change is easy to manipulate.'

This sort of style, in which criticism was distinctly muted, was normal in those days. It reflected the reactions of people who were more pleased by the convenience of two doors than worried about the length of the gearlever or the fact that the pedals were cramped. Such criticism would not become more intense until there was more competition. *The Autocar* went on:

'For the actual steering of the car we have unstinted praise; it is light and steady, the sense of direction is accurate, and it would be difficult to improve on it in any way.'

Such a statement might seem amazing to anybody who has driven an Austin Seven today, but it just goes to show how much cars have improved and it is possible to better seemingly impeccable engineering. But there was a discreet warning in *The Autocar*'s next comment: 'Light in action, the plate clutch takes up its work smoothly; there is, however, a very short travel on the pedal between engagement and disengagement.'

Without a speedometer, or access to proper timing apparatus, the performance could only be described (which did not matter much because there was little to compare with the Seven). *The Autocar* said:

'One of the most pleasing features of the car is the way in which it handles in traffic. Acceleration when using the gears is brisk, and the car can be manoeuvred rapidly in awkward places ... during the recent heat wave we took the Austin Seven over a succession of well-known hills in the Midland district and found that its hill-climbing capacity throughout was good. As is to be expected with small engines, an early change of gear on hills, so that the engine can maintain a high rate of revolutions, is necessary to get the best results...

'We were not altogether surprised to find that boiling took place during the ascent of the steep hills, but it must be added that on this particular trial car no fan was fitted and the amount of water lost was not great.'

Motorists in the 1920s expected to spend a lot more time keeping their cars running than they do today. Filling the radiator from wayside streams was commonplace, even adjusting the brakes during a long journey. But the braking system of the Austin Seven seems to have taxed even *The Autocar*'s powers of understatement:

'We carried out one or two tests of the brakes when descending various hills, and found that on the steep part of Willersey Hill neither brake independently would pull the car to a standstill with the clutch disengaged, but both brakes together would achieve the necessary result. In other words, the braking system should be equal to all demands on it.'

The Austin Seven received a similarly good reception from *The Autocar*'s weekly rival, *The Motor*, which went to some length in September 1923 to describe what a good second car it would make; or a good car anyway if you could afford only one:

'The Austin Seven is one of the most interesting miniature cars. In silent running, hill-climbing, acceleration and average speed it can hold its own with a big car, principally owing to the fact that the whole of the chassis and body is designed in harmony with the dimensions of the engine, and so produces a power-weight ratio of which many larger cars might be proud. Only in carrying capacity is the Seven at a disadvantage with the big car, and even then, considering that the overall dimensions of the vehicle are not much larger than those of a double bed, two grown-ups are really comfortably accommodated, while three children or their equivalent in luggage, parcels, cricket bags, gun cases, golf clubs, or fishing tackle can be housed in the space between the adjustable front sets and the back panel of the body, and at the same time can be protected by the hood.'

Wilmot Breeden's Calormeter on the radiator filler cap provided a good indication of when it was necessary to take on more water from a wayside stream, like *The Autocar*'s scribes.

What jolly boating weather ... the Dinghy of the Road made a Wonderful Auxiliary in the eyes of *The Motor*.

Such odd turns of phrase served only to illustrate that the people *The Motor* expected to buy the Austin Seven were mostly well-heeled. They went as far as to describe it as The Dingy of the Road and a Wonderful Auxiliary, before adding:

'On the road one is immediately impressed with the extraordinary acceleration of this tiny car and the manner in which it scuttles along winding tracks and up and down hill at speeds which make the legal limit seem slow... A trifle inclined to bounce on bad roads, when lightly laden, it makes up for this characteristic by arrowlike directness on good surfaces... When travelling at 40 mph the application of both brakes reduced the car to a standstill in about 40 yds, without any tendency to waltz or jump.'

The mind boggles as to what *The Motor* thought the Austin Seven might do. But *The Light Car and Cyclecar* were on hand to sum up on the earliest Sevens in February 1924:

'We were present about two years ago when the first Austin Seven made its bow to a critical but expert little gathering at the Austin works near Birmingham. The future of the little car then appeared very problematical. We noted that in every possible respect it was a large car in miniature—in some details, in fact, its specification was actually more complete than many large medium-priced cars.

'The four-wheel brakes were a case in point; these had never before been incorporated in the design of a baby car, and there were many other features seldom found on any but costly machines. Among these may be cited worm-and-sector steering, forced lubrication, throttle and magneto controls on the steering wheel, and stove enamel finish.

'We were told by Sir Herbert Austin when the first car made its debut that it had been introduced to supercede the sidecar combination; to seat more people in comfort than that comparatively unmechanical vehicle, and withal to be of only slightly greater overall size, thus requiring no larger garage accommodation.

'We have just concluded a week's trial of one of the latest Austin Sevens. During this period the car has covered a trifle more than 600 miles. Over this mileage no trouble of any kind was experienced, while if the average speed were calculated it would be found to be slightly in excess of the legal limit.

'In the hands of the average owner who did not concern himself with keeping the engine in the best possible tune, the Austin Seven should always be capable of at least 40 mph, whilst petrol consumption would not exceed 45 mpg. Oil consumption is negligible.

'Seated in the car there is plenty of legroom. The windscreen is arranged so that a driver of average height looks through the centre of the upper panel, and the steering wheel is most comfortably disposed when the adjustable driving seat is fixed approximately in the midway position.

'The pedals could not be better placed, but a little discomfort is caused due to there being no room to the left of the clutch pedal, where one's foot can be placed when not driving in traffic. The handbrake comes nicely to hand, but it is necessary to lean forward to grasp the gear lever and feel that it is well under control...

'With both front seats occupied there is a slight shortage of elbow room when heavy driving coats are being worn, but this is less noticeable when the all-weather equipment is stowed.'

With both front seats occupied, there is a slight shortage of elbow room when heavy driving coats are being worn, *The Light Car* and *Cyclecar* noted.

Such comments were, of course, common in the days before heaters, and when it was quite normal to wear a great deal of protective clothing before you ventured out in a motor car. And then, so attired, you would normally have the hood down, with plenty of room for elbows to hang over the sides of the sidescreen-less car. *The Light Car*, as this august journal was known to everybody, continued:

'The hood is neat in appearance, it is easily raised and lowered, and makes a firm weatherproof joint with the top of the windscreen. The side panels are rigid and readily secured to the doors with which they open. When in place the forward part of the side panels where they are attached to the windscreen uprights does not cause the objectionable blind spot so often found with these fittings.

'The steering is light and comfortable to handle all speeds, and there is no suspicion of tailwag even when traversing pot-holed roads at more than 30 mph.'

The frequent references to potholes in this test and others emphasised the quality of Britain's minor roads at the time and how well-suited the Austin

The hood is neat in appearance and makes a firm weatherproof joint with the windscreen, *The Light Car* discovered.

Seven was to such surfaces. *The Light Car* did not feel so secure about the brakes, but added that perhaps the linings were not fully bedded-in before going on:

'The travel of the clutch is rather short, but with practice it can be engaged extremely smoothly. As with the clutch, so with the gear lever, but the short travel is troublesome only when changing down from top to second and when a double-clutch change is necessitated by a moderately high road speed. When moving the gear lever into the neutral position in these circumstances it is too easy accidentally to overshoot neutral and jolt the second-gear pinions together. It would seem that some form of partial locking device would be an improvement. With a little practice we found, however, that a clean change could be made from top to second at speeds up to 25 mph.'

When next *The Autocar* tested an Austin Seven, in August 1924, they were most impressed with the modifications that had been made, although these did not, of course, include the brakes or clutch action. It was the revised lines that most appealed to the journalists. They found them a 'vast improvement' and liked the car so much that 'the satisfied driver wanted to administer appreciative pats on the side of the body.' Horses were still a common sight in Britain ... as was the Saturday-night 'hop' or village-hall dance: 'To borrow the phraseology of one of those popular modern song fox trots, the Austin Seven is a pony which keeps its tail up.' And then, casting pop journalism aside, *The Autocar* added:

'Since we tested the Austin Seven last year, an electric starter for the engine has been added, and it naturally makes the vehicle much nicer to handle when shopping or in wet weather.'

There's nothing new about wet weather, but it was most unpleasant having to get out in a downpour to start the car. And as for shopping, in those days you drove from shop to shop. Parking problems were almost unknown other than, perhaps, in the centre of a really big city. The position of the starter button took some getting used to, though, as *The Autocar* found:

'It is placed by the side of the starter body to the left of the driver's foot on the ramp board, and requires a little manoeuvring to be reached until one gets used to its position.

'So far as the road performance is concerned, a general improvement in the briskness is to be observed... On second gear the acceleration is phenomenally good, and by intelligent use of the gear box this car can be made to give a run to many a larger vehicle. We did, however, rather gain the impression that the extra liveliness of the engine had been obtained by the use of a higher compression, for we found that the slow running or acceleration on top gear was accompanied by a tendency on the part of the engine to thump, which retardation of the ignition ameliorated, but at the same time reduced the pulling powers over much.'

No changes to engine specification were recorded after the increase in bore, so exactly which power unit this car used must remain a mystery. It had shock absorbers on the front axle, however, which *The Autocar* found improved the steering. Similar comments were made by *The Motor* when they tested a Sports model, complete with speedometer, in January 1925:

The Motor found the performance of the 1924 Sports model to be quite astonishing.

'The performance of this little car on the road is astonishing, its remarkable acceleration, ability to maintain 40 mph or 50 mph, stability, lightness of steering and comfortable suspension being its principal features. In traffic its nimbleness, combined with its four-wheel braking system and diminutive proportions, makes it faster than any other form of road travel.'

That might have been taking it a bit far, but *The Motor* was right when it said:

'The fitting of shock absorbers renders the car steady on corners and independent of indifferent road surfaces, so that one can drive with as much dash and feeling of safety as one would adopt with a much larger car...

'The engine can be revved up through its entire range without any feeling of vibration or of extending it beyond its capabilities. Even prolonged hill-climbing on second and bottom gears cannot disturb the even tenor of its running, the fan-cooled radiator showing no sign of steaming after several miles on the lower gears.'

Thank goodness Sir Herbert had relented with this extra piece of metal now that there was a sports car. And now that it had a speedometer, the performance figures were interesting: maximum speed was quoted at 52 mph, with 41.5 mph obtainable in second gear. Minimum speeds in these ratios were 6 mph (top) and 5 mph (second). Fuel consumption worked out at 40 mpg on this hard-used example, more than 50 mpg having been obtained by less-sporting drivers. No performance figures were taken when the new monthly magazine *Motor Sport* tried a Gordon England Super-Sports Austin Seven, but the description of the way it went on a 'pet' testing course was enough:

'The first hill was approached by a blind right-hand bend, and though the driver had no previous knowledge of the somewhat tricky turn, his quick manipulation of the gear showed that the Austin is certainly very handy to control. In fact, at this early stage of the test it appeared as if there was at least 20 hp available under the bonnet, instead of a modest seven.

'Part of the course included some long straight stretches, with a very rough surface, and this provided an excellent test for the suspension system when travelling at high speed. On one occasion the rear springs "bottomed" over a double pot-hole, but as the combined weight of the passengers amounted to well over 23 stone, this could not be wondered at. Subsequently, I discovered that the rear shock absorbers were adjusted rather too tightly, which undoubtedly had some influence on the suspension generally.'

Not even motoring scribes could be expected to be technicians in those days, but *Motor Sport* went on in excellent vein:

'Hedsor Hill is somewhat deceptive as a brake testing gradient, for the sharp turn half way down necessitates the sudden application of the brakes, but the car was kept well in control by the use of front and rear brakes alternatively, even when making a very fast descent. On this particular car, it appeared that the brakes were a little fierce in action, probably due to want of a good run-in, but otherwise I could make no adverse comment.

'I took over the wheel at Bisham and being well acquainted with the hard climb to Winter Hill, wondered if the Austin would require a spell of bottom gear. At the foot of this hill I dropped into second gear and the rev. counter immediately went up to 3,500, which dropped slightly on rounding the hairpin bend. At first it seemed as if bottom gear would be needed, but I had underestimated the Austin acceleration, for on getting into the straight again, on the next part of the climb, the revolutions rose to just over 4,000, thus enabling me to use top gear before the summit was reached.

'The greasy surface at the hairpin bend seemed to present great opportunities for a first-class skid, but though I actually tried one, the little car kept to its even course and refused to oblige even with the slightest suspicion of tailwag.

'Though the car was not obviously intended for colonial conditions, I could not resist the temptation of trying it at a "stunt" hill in the neighbourhood. I think that this particular hill is very little known at present...

'Perhaps I was guilty of attempting the first part of the climb at too high a speed, as unfortunately one of the wheels slipped into a water course, which pulled the car up with a jerk. As this occurred at the very steepest part of the climb, it was intended to run down and try again; but on making an attempt to get away, I found to my surprise, that with the aid of the bottom gear, the car pulled itself out with ease and finished the climb on top without the least sign of distress.

'On concluding the test for hill climbing, the return journey was made over good roads, which gave the opportunity of judging how the car would behave under ordinary fast touring conditions. At a speed of 50 mph, it seemed as if one could keep on driving forever without fatigue, though naturally one has to become accustomed to the difference between driving a miniature car and one of the ordinary dimensions.

'Whilst it holds the road admirably, the Austin sports is distinctly lively, but gives no suggestion of the "pea on a drum" effect of which it is sometimes unjustly accused.'

The first Austin Seven saloon was to receive an equally enthusiastic reception in *The Autocar* in August 1926:

'We have made a test of this new Austin saloon and have been completely fascinated by it. It proves to be a perfectly practical miniature closed coach, superior in numerous important respects to many much larger and more expensive saloons... The finish is commendable; it is easy to secure adequate ventilation without draught, and the body is watertight, free both from fumes and from drumming.

'The application of a saloon body to the 7 hp chassis has made surprisingly little difference to the car's road performance and the saloon exhibits the same liveliness, the same tendency to overtake larger cars on hills, and the same extraordinary handiness in heavy traffic as is experienced with the touring model.

The Autocar viewed the first Austin Seven saloon as being a 'perfectly practical miniature closed coach'.

The car that made the Austin Seven's reputation complete ... the Top Hat saloon.

The tourer continued in basically similar form to the saloon, this 1926 example having been owned by the noted Austin Seven enthusiast Colin Chapman until his death.

'Steering is light, the springing is particularly comfortable, and the car holds the road so well that there is no necessity, even when travelling quickly, to pick a way between potholes. The controls are very light, and there is a refinement in the general running of the car very much greater than that which the price would lead one to expect.'

If only a modern car could land itself such an accolade, even though most might pale at the potholes that the Austin Seven traversed. The Gordon England fabric saloon proved uncommonly good at such tests when *The Autocar* subjected one to the Land's End Trial in 1927. Its crew considered that its equipment could not be bettered 'including as it does a single-piece front screen, pneumatic Scaco seats, a blind for the rear window, an interior lamp, and a useful ashtray.'

The car fared well on the trial, climbing everything the organisers could find, before its occupants set off back to London. On arrival, they analysed the cost of the run and discovered that six gallons of fuel were used on the outward 317 miles and eight while cruising faster on the return route of 298 miles; total cost less than 80p! Their analysis went on:

'Another thing was the extreme comfort of the car, for at no time in those 600-odd miles did either of the crew leave his seat to stretch himself, as one does after several hours on most cars. The suspension is very good indeed by comparison with other cars on the same route. Actually, many

Mulliner was among the coachbuilders which produced special bodies for the Austin Seven.

The one-piece windscreen gives a view that cannot be bettered, said *The Autocar*.

would prefer more castor action for the axle to give the little machine a better sense of direction, the position of the oil filler is not convenient, and the fuel tank filler, if one is careless, overflows directly over the engine. This is the sum total of searching criticism. As refinements more movement for the clutch pedal, and, possibly, the softening of the roughness at full throttle and low speed.

'Reliability, cooling, brakes, and general tractability are excellent. Not a squeak or rattle developed, not a nut was loose—and it had been a gruelling test—nor did the engine need decarbonising or attention. Undoubtedly the fabric body is a great attraction and wonderfully useful for ordinary work. Its silence is remarkable, it is easy to clean, and keeps its condition better than metal and paint. The one-piece windscreen gives a view that cannot be bettered, and the sliding windows are ideal if they have the stops which are fitted to later models to clamp the panes. More ventilation would be desirable on a really hot day, either a roof ventilator or provision for opening the front screen; anything, in fact, to allow a straight-through draught to be arranged easily when the occupants feel like experiencing one.'

As we were saying, journalists in those days could be masters of understatement, for this test took place at Easter rather than in the height of summer. Perhaps with those comments in mind, *The Autocar* was given a second Gordon England fabric saloon to test a year later. This time it had a sunshine roof, and they reported:

'It is certain that there is a great future for the sunshine saloon—a type of body consistently fostered by this journal—and the England model is not only of very simple construction, but it does definitely give one a waterproof closed car for bad weather and a freely-ventilated, wholly open, car in good weather. From inside it would be impossible to tell that there is anything out of the ordinary about the body. There is no sign of any extra mechanism, nor does the roof appear to be other than that usually used in a saloon.

'The roof consists of a long piece of fabric attached to the body only at the back, but secured to it all round the edge by a number of press buttons. It takes, therefore, a little over a minute for two people to unclip the buttons, roll up the top and fasten it in position at the back by the two straps provided. Similarly, it is just as easy to put it back again into position.

'With the roof open the car is quieter; snug, yet airy, and the view of the surrounding country, especially in mountain passes, is entirely unimpeded. Since the fabric overlaps the sides of the body, it is not in the least likely that this design will leak. The real problem is whether press buttons are sufficiently durable for the average driver who is inclined to treat this method of attachment roughly. It is also essential that the fabric should not stretch or shrink, for if it did so the buttons could not be secured. This criticism is met by the statement that the type of press button

The sunshine roof came in for a lot of praise from *The Autocar* whether in its closed or open position, although care was advised with the press-stud retaining buttons.

is specially chosen for the purpose and that, after all, in case of trouble it would be a very small job to replace one button or more.

'It might be thought that the diagonal bracing members across the open roof would be rather in the way, but in fact they are not, and the only point is that they should be trimmed with some material that will stand rain, for it is inevitable that the car will be driven with the roof open in rain at some time or another . . .

'This type of saloon is better ventilated than most of the others, because there is a special ventilator above the single-piece windscreen.'

The Motor did not comment on the ventilation at great length when they tested a tourer in February 1929, except to say that the ingenious sidescreens could be opened or closed to 'exactly the right degree required.'

The Autocar noted that the tourer's hood could be lowered . . . and the sidescreens opened . . . to just the right degree.

The Autocar's plea for an opening front screen was heeded on the 1928 fabric saloon.

They noted, however, that only 'very slight alterations to the shock absorbers will make considerable difference to the suspension.' Performance figures were taken carefully, which resulted in a top speed of 52 mph being recorded, with a minimum speed in top gear, ignition fully retarded, of only 6 mph. Fuel consumption also came under close scrutiny, with more than 50 mpg being possible if only the driver was on board and the speed restricted to 25 mph; at the worst, with vigorous driving and two adults, the consumption should never fall below 40 mpg, said *The Motor*.

Similar performance figures were recorded by *The Autocar* when they tested a tourer two months later, with significant comments on the coil ignition and its pot-holing ability: *The Autocar* said:

'The latest model seems to run more smoothly, especially at lower speeds. This tendency may be due to the coil ignition now fitted in place of the magneto. The new system is more sensitive to the use of the advance and retard control.

'For trial, a sample of the touring model was taken out; it was a fairly new car with only about 500 miles to its credit, so that the initial stiffness had hardly worn off. The way in which the car hums steadily along main roads at a sweet 40 mph is rather marvellous, for this figure represents its natural cruising speed. Another outstanding feature is its handiness and quickness in traffic, by reason of which capabilities it nips along in a fashion denied to larger vehicles. Since last year, by the way, the steering column has been lengthened and a relatively flat steering wheel takes the place of the old dished type, so that there is more knee room for a tall driver, a point many will appreciate.

'It cannot be expected that a small car can be made to ride so entirely

The Autocar found that the open Austin Seven rode extremely well for its size even in the most arduous tests.

comfortably as a large one, but, on the other hand, the Seven rides extraordinarily well for its size. In this matter, the latest type of springs and the back and front shock absorbers materially help, for the hold on the road is better than was the case with early models. It was found possible to drive steadily over a road deeply indented with severe potholes, over which considerably larger cars have been known to "buck".

'One of the features of the design is the clever way in which it is arranged so that persons of widely varying heights can make themselves comfortable in the driving seat, the latter being adjustable fore and aft when the cushion is raised to disclose a stop. The front bucket seats themselves are very comfortable and carry support well up the back. The pedal movement is unusually short, but quite light, and the clutch is sufficiently gentle.'

The modifications that had been made to the Austin Seven over the years also received an accolade from *The Light Car* in January 1930:

'Of all the pioneers of small cars, Sir Herbert Austin must surely be given the credit of being one of the most far-sighted and courageous. With absolute confidence he launched, some eight years ago, a type of vehicle which was quite new in the world of light cars, and that confidence was not misplaced, for the public at once took to the attractive little Seven and within a few months of its debut it began to be seen here, there and everywhere. Most astonishing of all, perhaps, is the fact that since 1922 no radical alterations have been made in the general layout of the car, whilst externally it is almost exactly the same as the first example which passed through the gates of the great works at Longbridge.

'From time to time, however, improvements in detail have been incorporated, but these have not been "seasonal"—that is to say, they have not been advertised as an improvement in the ensuing year's models. On the contrary, these modifications have been made as and when they appeared desirable; hence it is that, with the 1929 Show still fresh in our memory, the Austin Seven appears with a longer gearlever. A small improvement, but what a difference it makes to the comfort of handling the car—as we discovered when, a few days ago, following a tour of the Longbridge works, we took over one of the latest coachbuilt saloons for a test run . . .

'The particular saloon placed at our disposal was practically new; at any rate, it had only 200 miles to its credit when we turned towards the fine open country beyond the gates of the Longbridge works. At the outset we appreciated the new position of the starter button—just behind the gearbox—and also the rearrangement of the selector mechanism. First gear is now near-side back, second gear off-side forward, and top off-side back.

'With top and second on the driver's side, and a longer lever, gear changing calls for movement only of the left arm. One does not have to

The Light Car noted that the 1930 saloon and tourer hardly changed in appearance over the years.

move one's position in the driving seat, whilst when in top gear the ball which surmounts the gear lever practically touches the driver's left knee, where the hand falls on to it quite naturally and with certainty.'

If the driving position was cramped, the style certainly wasn't ... and *The Autocar* continued in similar vein when testing a factory sunshine saloon in March 1931:

'Some of the later modifications have made a big improvement in the control, while others are a matter of detail. For instance, the long gear lever

The sporting Austins, heralded by this 1927 Super Sports model, received very good reviews from the testers.

is exactly right and free from whip, and though the ball-type change might suggest increased difficulty for the unskilled driver as compared with the old visible gate, the latest change is certainly easier to handle. The steering, too, while as light as ever, is more definite, though there is still no castor action... Especially with more than one person in the car, there is a marked absence of the fore-and-aft movement formerly noticeable on certain road surfaces, though to secure this effect, comfort has not been sacrificed.

'Again, the brakes are now connected so that the shoes on both front and back wheels are applied by either the pedal or the lever, and this is a change for the better... A lesser, but important, control which also is more convenient is the hand-operated starting switch.'

It was at about this time that a series of tests took place on the unsupercharged version of the Ulster that Austin were hoping would sell well. *The Motor* had the first opportunity in July 1930 and waxed lyrical:

'First and foremost it should be stated that, despite the very modest chassis dimensions ... there is ample accommodation in the body for two full-sized adults. The writer, himself a six-footer, can sit right into the body and with ample legroom be quite comfortable at the wheel for long periods at a stretch. Furthermore, the high squab, which, by the way, is no less than 23 ins deep, gives just the right amount of support to the shoulders that is so necessary in a fast car. Again, the body width of 36 ins is sufficient for driver and passenger to sit "separately" as it were, a hummock in the

The 1930 Ulster became one of the favourite Austin Sevens.

centre of the upholstery for the squab enabling lateral location for the occupants of the seats to be obtained when the car is being cornered at a fast pace.

'Mention should also be made of the arrangement of the controls. A new and longer lever enables the driver to change gear without leaning forward in the slightest degree, while the rake of the steering column has been so adjusted that it fits nicely into the lap without being in the way when entering or leaving the car—there are no doors in this Austin Sports model...

'As soon as the engine started it was apparent that it had plenty of what is often loosely termed "pep"—an impression afterwards borne out in fact. When it is realised that the unit delivers 24 bhp at 5,000 rpm and the complete car weighs but 8½ cwt unladen the raison d'etre for the brisk performance becomes obvious. Naturally such high revolution speeds call for large induction passages, and it would be unreasonable to expect a very good power output at low rates of revolutions. For this reason we were unable to start our acceleration tests from a datum of 10 mph; at 15 mph, however, the engine fired with perfect regularity and accelerated excellently throughout the whole range.'

Although the car was brand new, with only 10 miles recorded when the test started (and only another 150 miles during the test), *The Motor* still managed to reach 62 mph in top gear. At first glance, their acceleration graph might seem strange by today's standards, because no figures were recorded from a standstill. It was revealed, for instance, that it took 25 seconds to reach 50 mph from 10 mph, using second gear only, and that first gear in the Sports models close-ratio gearbox could be held to 30 mph, with a 52 mph maximum in second. So why didn't *The Motor* record a 0–50 mph time using first and second gears, or a 0–60 mph time using all three? The reason was that traffic lights were few and far between in those days and speeds of more than 30 mph might have resulted in a reckless driving charge in the towns in which they were situated. Such times from a standstill were also less relevant because the more common situation would have been to have become stuck behind some slow-moving traffic and wish to accelerate past—probably without changing gear. Heavy vehicles in those days often moved at only 10 or 15 mph, and lorries were limited to 20 mph in any case. This test was also significant when analysed more than fifty years later, for the way in which *The Motor* were starting to use the term 'in' for riding in a car, rather than 'on'—as on horseback—which had been universal until that time. Their far-seeing scribe went on:

'The controls are all light to the touch and extremely easy to manipulate. Engagement of the clutch, for example, is quite a simple matter providing one realises that the pedal travel is rather short. The gears can be engaged, either upwards or downwards, without the driver having to worry about gauging the relative speed of the meshing pinions with accuracy...' Such were the pleasures of a close-ratio box. *The Motor* continued:

'As might be expected in a car with an engine capable of such high revolution speeds, one uses the indirect ratios far more than on a normal touring type of car...

'The car really comes into its own on the open road, for there, with the throttle open wide and a pleasant buzz emanating from the fishtail of the exhaust system, one really feels quite a thrill of speed. It is not easy to give an exact ideal cruising pace because the car seems to settle down quite comfortably at any rate of travel between 35 mph and 60 mph . . .

'Summing up, this Austin sports model should appeal particularly to that very enthusiastic class of driver who desires high performance with economy. Although driven hard during our test, the consumption worked out at 30.5 mpg (a meritorious figure for a brand-new car) and the oil consumption was almost negligible.'

Motor Sport's version had covered hardly any more miles when it was tested in the same year, but managed 37.5 mpg over a variety of roads. The new monthly journal agreed with *The Motor*, except that its braking figures were not quite so good—it took 130 ft to stop the car from 40 mph, whereas *The Motor* managed such a distance from 50 mph. But *Motor Sport* went on to say: 'The deceleration was steady and comfortable, although the rear brakes tended to come on before the front ones. This, however, was a matter of simple adjustment.' Obviously, this adjustment, by means of a wing nut, was critical. *The Light Car* was equally delighted with their non-supercharged Ulster when they drove it in May 1931, their comments on the gear ratios—which had been lowered overall to increase performance—being particularly significant:

'The high compression . . . engine started very easily and quickly without the starting handle having to be used, the electric starter being well able to spin the crankshaft, although heavy "R" grade oil was used.

'A peculiarity of the engine is that in spite of its high compression it is by no means particular about its fuel, having no tendency to pink. At 5,000 rpm, it gives 24 bhp and a speed of 28.2 mph in bottom, 50.5 mph in second and 72 mph in top. We found that this maximum top-gear speed could be reached only under very favourable conditions, the normal maximum being about 64 mph, and 60 mph always being within comfortable reach.

'This little Sports Austin will, in fact, tour at between 55 mph and 60 mph indefinitely, running extremely sweetly, holding the road perfectly and averaging 36 mpg of petrol with a negligible oil consumption. On second gear its performance is good. It will jump from 10 to 40 mph in 14 seconds and continue to accelerate cleanly and progressively up to well over 50 mph still in second. From a standing start, using the gears, 50 mph can be reached in 24 seconds, a performance made possible by the exceptional snappiness of the engine and the very rapid gear changes which can be effected . . .

'On all normal hills extremely fast ascents can be made in second gear, but a drop to bottom is needed for the sterner stuff one meets in Devonshire.

'Freak hills, unless taken exceedingly fast, cannot be conquered on the 13.5:1 bottom gear. We found Porlock was easily climbed, however; also the very stiff climb from Babbacombe Beach to the top of the cliff. Beggar's Roost, however, called for a lower gear, the well-known hump being safely negotiated but causing so many revs to be lost that the car came to a standstill a short distance above it.

'For trials work, with a slightly lower bottom gear, the car would, however, be almost ideal, having a splendid steering lock, good brakes, and that sturdiness and willingness which are such important attributes.'

The Autocar enthused over the Austin Seven Sports when it tested one in June 1931, although they did not go as far as to take acceleration figures from a standstill. Their data was from 10 mph and similar to that recorded by *The Motor*, a maximum speed of 66 mph over a standing quarter mile being more directly comparable with the figures relating to modern cars. But *The Autocar* summed up very aptly why the Sports model was so attractive, saying:

'The whole feel of the car is very different from what is associated with the standard touring types. To begin with, the frame and front axle are appreciably lower, the springs are bound with cord to stiffen them, which combined factors give the car a genuine feeling of stability even when corners are taken fast. Further, the stiffening of the suspension, apart from its practical aspect, helps to increase the sports car effect.'

The Autocar reflected the sporting style of the day in which steering wheels were worn very close to the chest, by commenting: 'The driving position is comfortable, though it seems at first as though the wheel could be closer. The point that really counts in this direction is that after a very long run the driver is not at all tired or cramped.' It would be 25 years or more before steering wheels generally adopted today's position where the arms are freely extended, although this Austin was part of the way there in 1930. But the way in which the brakes were best operated was distinctly vintage:

'The brake action, again, is light, and there is never any tendency for the car to deviate from its course; although it is now arranged that either the pedal or the hand lever applies the shoes on all four wheels, in an emergency stop the effect can be increased by employing both pedal and lever.'

No matter that it was necessary to take one hand off the steering wheel in such a manoeuvre ... *Motor Sport* also showing no such inhibitions over control when they tested an even more interesting sporting Austin Seven in 1930. Their comments on a Boyd-Carpenter 'B.C.' Austin being particularly illuminating:

'The first and most obvious departure from standard is the body. This is a two-seater of very attractive appearance, stiff construction, and, what is unusual on a very small sports car, really adequate luggage capacity. It is a truism that the people who travel in small cars are just as large, and require just as much luggage as those who traverse the country in larger vehicles. Yet in spite of this it is regrettably rare to find a small car with reasonable equipment in this respect. In the B.C. Austin, however, there is ample room in the well-planned tail for all that any two normal beings are likely to require, in the way of suitcases, golf clubs, fishing rods, and what-not.

'The spare wheel is carried on the side of the body, and while enhancing the appearance, is also prevented from getting mixed up with articles which will suffer thereby. Spare wheels may be beautifully clean and smart when they leave the works, but the one which has just been removed from its workaday position owing to its inability to hold air, is usually far from it, and the side of the car seems to be the obvious place for it.

'As far as mechanical details are concerned, it at once becomes evident that the firm have applied their very considerable racing experience with great effect, and it is hard to find any particular area where further tuning could be carried out.

'The car tested was one of the overhead-valve conversions, but as far as other points on the chassis go, the same remarks apply to all models. The head in question has been specially designed to fit on the standard engine with as little structural alteration as possible, and can be fitted to any standard Austin Seven in a matter of two days, or changed back to the normal side valve job in one. The valves are operated by push rods, which run in the old valve guides, and the head is so arranged as to blank off the old ports, while an extension fitted to the old manifold enables this to be used in the conversion. The resulting engine looks perfectly normal and bears no stamp that it has been converted, such as is the case with some other overhead valve "fitments," which we have seen in the past.

'Other details include the fitting of a special Claudel Hobson carburettor, opening and polishing the ports (probably one of the most tedious jobs an amateur can undertake), lowering the springs and consequently the chassis, and fitting extra leaves, lowering and extending the steering to give a proper "scrapping" position, and altering the gear change. This is effected by mounting the gear lever well aft of the box on an additional cross member, and coupling it to the gear box by a horizontal rod with yoke ends, which thus transmits both fore-and-aft and lateral motion to the standard gearshift arrangement. The additional convenience when driving has to be experienced to be believed, as one's left hand drops directly on to the lever, and changes can be effected in the middle of the most complicated evolutions, which is a great help when cornering. Cornering is very steady, due to the lowered centre of gravity, and the steering is positive and accurate, though we should have personally preferred it to be slightly more self-centreing.

'The car which we tried had seen some fairly violent service in competitions over a considerable period, and had many successes to its credit. Owing·to the fact that its life as a competition car, combined with demonstrations, had made it impossible to give it the attention which a privately-owned vehicle would have received, there were one or two small points which could not be fairly criticised. The brakes were really in need of relining, so that the stopping distance of 84 ft from 40 mph does not really represent what can be done with this model. A good feature of the braking system is the large outside lever, which in the latest models operates all four sets of shoes, and is placed in just the right position. In fact, during the time we had this car for test we found it most convenient to drive almost exclusively on the hand brake. This car has actually covered the flying kilometre at 78 mph, but the maximum speed reached while in our hands was 71 mph, due chiefly to the fact that the engine had no attention for some thousands of miles, and although it did not show any signs of getting tired on long runs, it is well known that such a small engine requires reasonably frequent decarbonisation if it is to maintain its maximum performance.

'Second gear provided very snappy acceleration and was of great assistance in putting up high average speeds over a twisty cross country route. Between 50 and 55 mph was possible in this gear, while the engine balance at high speeds was perfect. At low speeds there was a slight tendency to roughness if made to pull hard, but this is only what one would expect, and in any case such a vehicle is not meant to be driven at a crawl on top gear. Provided, however, that the revs are kept up, the top gear performance is remarkably good, and hills which would call for a change of gear on a standard Seven could be taken in its stride at a rousing speed; while if an obstruction occurred, second gear was more than adequate to regain the lost speed, and pass any normal car.'

The Light Car also had the opportunity to test a B.C. Austin Seven in March 1930, although it was brand-new and capable of only 62 mph—which was impressive enough for them to write:

'These comparatively high speeds were only matched in fascination by the really exceptional roadholding qualities of the car. Except in pukka sports cars—replicas of road-racing machines—we do not expect to find roadholding such as this. On fast and slow bends, the B.C. Austin behaved with a like steadiness and with an inside wheel bounding over bumps in the gutter the car showed no signs of bucking, nor did the steering wheel jerk or shudder in the hands. On the straight, with the throttle propped open, the steering was finger-light and the car could be held easily with one hand. As a matter of fact, the car was driven all-out "hands off", with no tendency to deviate from the set course.

'High averages are easy in the B.C. Austin, as ordinary bends and corners can be taken with complete safety at speeds far higher than is normal, and with such an excellent performance in second, allied with very good brakes—which pulled the car neither from one side nor the other— mile after mile could be reeled off at averages of well over 35 mph.'

The next round of tests concerned the new long-wheelbase saloon, which received universal acclaim from the 'Big Three' weekly magazines. *The Motor* commented of their test, in November 1931:

'Two adults of average stature can be accommodated with comfort to such a degree that even long journeys would not become arduous. Wells on each side of the propellor shaft, and extending under the front seats, accommodate the feet, and there is sufficient knee room to prevent any cramped feeling ... while the rear squab adequately supports the shoulders. It will thus be appreciated that a considerable improvement has been made in the accommodation available in this model.

'New pattern wings enhance the appearance and effectively protect the bodywork from mud, as we had adequate opportunity to discover, most of our test being carried out in bad weather...

'It is with particular interest that we tried this new model in order to see what effect the increase in weight, combined with the longer wheelbase, would have on performance.

'Roadholding and suspension are greatly improved, the car riding very well at speeds of 40 mph over rough road surfaces with notable smoothness. There is little pitching even on very bad surfaces, whilst higher up the scale, nearer to the maximum speed of 50 mph, there is hardly the slightest tendency to stray from a straight course. Controllability is a commendable feature even on wet and slippery surfaces...

'For a long run the happiest cruising speed appeared to be in the region of 40 mph, which can be held cheerfully for mile after mile...

'The excellent performance of this little car is partly attributable to the lowering of the rear axle ratio ... this permits the engine to rev more and thus develop more power. True, the safe limit on second gear is not quite so high, but in the face of the enhanced top gear performance this does not matter very much.'

The Motor then went on to record the most comprehensive performance figures of 50 mph flat out, 35 mph in second gear and 18 mph in first. Their 10–30 mph acceleration time was 22 seconds, 10–30 mph 37 seconds (the same as the sole standing-start time, for 0–40 mph, using all three gears) and 0–45 in 55 seconds. Fuel consumption was between 45 and 50 mpg. *The Light Car* managed to cut the critical 10–30 mph time in half by resorting to the use of second gear, but mentioned that only in passing in a welter of comment on the new body when they tested the long-wheelbase saloon three days later:

'The alteration [to the wheelbase] has resulted in a big improvement in every way. In the matter of appearance the difference is, perhaps, the least noticeable owing to the fact that the overall dimensions have been kept compact, the full length of the car having been increased by 2 ins only. The extra length has been added to the rear seat cushion. Having got so far, the reader might be tempted to think that the added length of the wheelbase is nothing to make a fuss about: why add 6 ins to the chassis and then use only two of them for the body is a justifiable question.

'The answer is rather lengthy and brings to light several advantages of the new model that are not obvious at first sight. In the first place, it is an established fact that, other things being equal, the longer the wheelbase, the more even will be the riding qualities over bumpy surfaces and the better will be the roadholding. That is advantage number one.

'Then, again, the nearer the seats are to the centre of the wheelbase, the greater the comfort. In the case of the new Austin, the placing of the rear axle farther back in relation to the body has virtually had the same effect as bringing the rear seats farther forward (i.e. nearer to the centre),

Austin Seven saloons pictured with and without louvres on their bonnets—received a great welcome from the road test teams.

so that a noticeable improvement in the comfort of the rear seats is obtained—advantage number two.

'The third advantage of the change is that it is now possible to arrange the doors clear of the wheelarch with a consequent improvement in the accessibility of the rear seats.'

The Light Car did show itself to be something of a pioneer when it commented bluntly: 'Our only criticism concerns the brakes, which, with the model we tried, could have been more powerful with advantage.'

The Autocar got over this problem in their test next month by adopting the sporting method of tugging on the handbrake at the same time as pressing the brake pedal, and countered a previous, heavily-veiled, criticism of the difference between the lighting on full beam and that on dipped by saying:

'The driving light is entirely adequate for the speed of the car; the dimming is effective and gives sufficient power to enable one to continue in safety, and is the kind of illumination, incidentally, which is useful in thick mist.'

But just to show that they were not wholly biased in favour of their advertisers, they pointed out: 'An oil pressure gauge has been fitted for some time past in place of the older tell-tale button, and in view of that alone the instruments should be lit for night driving.'

From around this time, even the most conservative of magazines would generally carry some small quibble with a car's composition, just to show that they really cared about their readers, amid a welter of words in which criticism was largely confined, between the lines, to the previous model. In this vein, *The Autocar* hinted at the claustrophobic nature of earlier Austin Seven saloons by saying: 'Not only is there more legroom in the back compartment and a greater width, so that two people of normal size can occupy the back seats more comfortably, but there is also greater space between the driver and the front passenger, which is very much better.'

But so far as the relative lack of performance data was concerned, they probably had their market summed up very well as they wrote:

'In dealing with the performance of the Austin Seven, the point that invariably comes uppermost is that with this car, more than with practically any other existing machine, the question of exact data concerning acceleration, speed, and so forth, is of far less significance than with other types of car.

'It does not matter to a mile or two an hour or fractions of a second what is the limit of speed, or the rapidity of acceleration over a given range. The Seven stands by itself; it has made its name, and it is an immense success because it is one of the lowest-priced cars available that is capable of carrying several people wherever they may wish to go, at a very low cost per mile and in comfort.'

As the vast majority of Austin Sevens continued to trundle along at between

25 and 35 mph while on the road, and a good deal slower when off the road, *The Light Car* decided to show just what a de luxe saloon could do in July 1932. Their 'road' test began with this great quote:

'"Man and boy, these 23 years, have I bin in these parts an' never afore have I seen a motorcar this fur up on the moor—an' such a little 'un, too!" So spake an Exmoor farmer when we were testing the new de luxe Austin Seven saloon. There were two objects in view. First, to prove that the Seven, even in its largest form, is definitely a go-anywhere car, and secondly, that it goes anywhere at the very minimum cost.

'It was in the course of a ramble across wildest Exmoor that we met this native of the West, and the point had been reached after an hour's climbing up moorland tracks, including the plunge through a hub-deep stream. No wonder, then, that he was amazed. The incident should have brought home to him the fact that no longer is it necessary to be dependent on horses for transport when living in outlandish places. In 1932 even the smallest and cheapest car can be used with perfect assurance by those living off the beaten track.

'And now this point of economy. On a weekend run, 775 miles were covered. This is a far greater distance in just over two days than most people would care to go, and it enabled most of the famous beauty spots of the West to be visited. The total amount spent on petrol and oil was under 28 s (£1.40p)! Middlesex, Buckinghamshire, Wiltshire, Somerset, Devon, Dorset and Surrey: seven counties laid out at one's feet in the weekend for an outlay of 28 s. What other form of transport can compare? This charge, by the way, can be spread over several persons—for this latest Austin provides accommodation for four full-sized occupants. During our test the load consisted of two and a large amount of heavy baggage, so that the car was carrying very nearly maximum weight...

'In one hour, 35 mph was clocked and in another 38 mph. Surely a remarkable performance. Later the main roads were forsaken for the

The de luxe saloon introduced in 1932 provided *The Light Car* with an extraordinary go-anywhere road and off-road test.

byways and an afternoon's exploring undertaken in North Somerset. The little car took well-known hills, such as Porlock and Lynmouth, in a brave fashion and only on some of the very much steeper acclivities in the heart of the moor was it necessary to shed the passenger.

'During these strenuous tests, the sun was pouring down relentlessly, so that the Austin may be forgiven for occasionally boiling...'

The tests that followed, by *The Light Car* and *The Autocar*, of the four-speed de luxe saloon late in 1932 gave the impression that their road testers had both been briefed by the same company representative. Nevertheless, *The Light Car*'s comments on the new ratios hinted at the compromise that had to be made, amid other detail:

'The starter was, naturally, the first point that came under notice and scored full marks straightaway; the new remote control is far more convenient than the old. One simply operates the strangler knob with the left hand, the starter knob with the right, tickles the accelerator pedal— and off she goes, however cold it may be. Incidentally, if the starter should fail there is a sensible, permanently fitted, starting handle instead of the usual awkward detachable affair.

'Full marks were also awarded to the new carburation and induction arrangements, as the strangler had to be used very little and the engine was pleasantly free from that spluttering and lack of power during the first mile or two that used to be rather troublesome.

'To return to first impressions, great care was taken in engaging the clutch on leaving the showrooms, as Austin Seven clutch pedals have a very short travel. Care proved to be unnecessary, as the latest clutches seem to give a smooth getaway, even if one is forgetful. Full marks again...'

And at last *The Light Car* got on to what was the most important part of the new car, the gearbox:

'On the score of easy changing, marks can undoubtedly be awarded as before, whilst the third speed is moderately silent. In the matter of ratios, however, there is room for two opinions. Top and third correspond very closely with the top and second of the old three-speed box, second is a little higher than the old bottom, whilst the new first speed is in the nature of an emergency ratio.

'In choosing these ratios, the makers undoubtedly had in mind the fact that many drivers dislike changing, and certainly do not want to be bothered with two changes (top to third and third to second) on hills of the 1-in-8 variety. The new box, therefore, has all the attractions of the old to these drivers, with the additional advantages of a very useful emergency ratio for restarting on an up-grade or tackling freak hills.

'On the other hand, a third ratio in the region of 7.5:1 would undoubtedly prove a boon for moderately heavy traffic or main-road hills that are just too steep for top; but as a third of this type would certainly mean more changing, the Austin plan is perhaps the better, bearing in mind the fact that so many people start their motoring career in a Seven!'

The rest of the comments were good, particularly about the ride . . . 'One of the passengers calmly poured out a cup of tea from a vacuum flask and drank it without spilling a drop at 30 mph.' You couldn't have done that on a horse . . .

The Autocar presented the official line about the ratios, and added:

'The four-speed gear box controls much more pleasingly than its three-speed forerunner, the lever being long; in fact it is so well placed that it is possible to change between top and third without removing the left hand from the steering wheel, though that may not be intended. Yet the lever does not whip, and with appreciable pauses in neutral on the upward changes, and with light, fairly quick movements in changing down, the action is very good indeed.'

They then went on to give illuminating performance figures of 10.5 seconds needed to proceed between 10 and 30 mph in third gear, 19 seconds in top, and 28 seconds from 20 to 40 mph in top, before adding about the other changes:

'One of the most important is the provision of a rear fuel tank . . . and another big improvement, to the interior, is the provision of a modern type of instrument panel which incorporates a proper oil pressure gauge as well as a gauge for the fuel tank; there is now a key for the ignition switch, which certainly tends to greater peace of mind when the car has to be left . . .'

The Light Car then followed up with a test of a standard two-seater which then sold at £105 as opposed to £128 for the de luxe saloon. As it stood, the tourer offered almost every facility of the saloon other than for the back seats and had the advantage of a cosy, but completely detachable, hood. *The Light Car* were thoroughly enamoured and said:

'Our experiences go to show that the Austin in its smallest and cheapest form is still one of the most attractive models in the range, and that it has a performance which is really entirely out of keeping with its size! Folk who are considering the two-seater are, in fact, sometimes inclined to be misled by the compact proportions of the vehicle, but two minutes in either the driver's or the passenger's seat will serve to convince them that the legroom and elbow room is as generous as that found in many another car in a larger class. When it is added that the Austin is easy to control and boasts of all the usual fittings and accessories it will be realised that it is a very delightful proposition indeed.'

Sales of the tourer were not high, however, because potential customers were more often able to afford the extra money for the extra seats—or fancied a more sporting car, such as the recently-introduced 65, or one of the special-bodied Austin Sevens that cost at least £150. To many, the appearance was at least as important as the performance, and *The Light Car* commented in their test of a 65 in June 1933:

'The general outline of the car is pleasing. Its curves are evidently the result of much thought. The top of the door—which, by the way, is commendably wide—follows a curve which matches nicely that of the lower edge of the body and the tail has a converse curve which blends well with the rear wings.

'Probably even more important is the fact that the body is a thoroughly practical job, being both comfortable and convenient. Taking the latter

The Light Car was most enthusiastic in 1933 about the lines of the Type 65.

point first, the rear panel is hinged and conceals not only the spare wheel but also the pump, wheel brace, jack and jack handle, each being properly fixed in position. Consequently, when changing a wheel it is not necessary to unpack all the other tools as well, these being carried in a large box under the bonnet.

'This spare wheel compartment is quite separate from the luggage space, which is reached from inside the body and is behind the two tip-up adjustable bucket seats. These are provided with Moseley Float-on-Air cushions and are most comfortable, while their height above the ground is only 14 ins. The width across the inside of the body incidentally, is just 40 ins, so that there is plenty of room.

'A neat envelope is provided for the hood, which folds into an inclined position. The Triplex safety-glass screen is also inclined and the single panel can be hinged upwards. A neat feature is the provision of a simple catch at each lower corner, so that when the screen is closed it is held firmly both at the top and the bottom.'

The Motor published a test of the same model in the same week which gave the impression that writers from the two magazines had tried the same car, their reports were so similar. At any rate, in each case a new car, which had yet to be run-in, achieved 63 mph on the speedometer, and *The Motor* said with some satisfaction: 'A noticeable feature was the unusual rigidity of the wings and headlamps, which did not vibrate at any speed.'

The Motor also noted a complete absence of vibration in the wings and headlights of their 65...

Six months later, when more 65s were in circulation, *The Light Car* were able to publish a more thorough test. After detailing all the changes from standard, they said:

'The effect of all these differences is to alter the feel of the car entirely, and when one takes the wheel there is no doubt that the car is a sports model. The getaway, for example, is much crisper than on the normal Seven, and the car has that rather tight feeling about the suspension that immediately suggests to the enthusiast that it will hold the road well at speed...

'It can be put into a corner fast with confidence that it will behave itself all the way round. There is no rolling and none of that unpleasant tendency to "yaw" out of the true course.

'Another pleasing feature is that the steering is reasonably high-geared, slightly over one turn of the wheel serving to put the front wheels from full lock one side to full lock the other. Although the car does not, in actual fact, show any great tendency to slide about on grease, this fairly high ratio gives the driver confidence that if it does skid there will be no trouble in getting it straight again.

'It might be thought from these remarks that the steering and suspension would be unpleasant in traffic, the former being stiff and the latter unyielding; actually there is no suggestion of either, the designers seeming to have combined touring and sporting characteristics very happily.

'With regard to performance, the getaway from a standstill is very good, the standing quarter mile being covered in 27 seconds. Moreover, the gear change is quite quick and is also very simple, owing, of course, largely to the use of constant-mesh pinions for the three top ratios. There is, therefore, every incentive to make full use of the gearbox, and on a twisty, winding lane the car is delightful to handle...

'Lest it be thought that, in their endeavours to improve the performance, the makers have spoilt the other characteristics of the engine, it may be added that starting is easy, the tickover is quite even and, throughout its range, the engine is fairly smooth, provided that suitable use is made of the ignition control. This latter point is important, because the car is very sensitive in this respect and can easily be over-advanced at low speeds, in which case roughness is noticeable.'

Motor Sport managed to test a distinctly unusual 65 in 1934—one fitted with an Arrow body by H.A. Saunders in North London. Their tester must also have been on the large side, because he found the car cramped when kitted out for cold weather with a driving rug across his knees. He reported:

'It goes without saying that a small engine must turn over rapidly to produce its power but the Austin ran smoothly and without vibration throughout its range, although not mounted on rubber. It was quite flexible too, running on number one petrol, but in order to get away quickly the gearbox had to be used freely. It was one of the best we have tried, with an easy and rapid change, and constant-mesh second and third gears. Third and top gears are fitted with synchromesh mechanism, an additional refinement rarely used. The clutch had a short travel, but took up the drive smoothly.

'The steering was high-geared and light, but without much castor action. This did not cause any difficulty as the wheel was easily centred, but a longer steering column would be appreciated by tall drivers, since at present the wheel rim is in contact with one's driving rug.

'The accelerator pedal is close to the brake, so that in an emergency stop it is possible to apply both at once. We therefore preferred to use the handlever which also operates the four brakes, and using a fair amount of force we were able to pull up from 40 mph in 62 ft without any deviation from the straight. The position of the steering wheel and accelerator could be altered without much difficulty, if they were found to be inconvenient.

'In spite of these minor annoyances, the car was definitely pleasing to handle for the driving position was good. The steering wheel and the gearlever were right under one's hand and the cutaway of the side of the body supported the right arm. With a short wheelbase car one can slip through traffic with the minimum of delay, while the lowered chassis allows corners to be taken in exhilarating fashion. It also seems to have improved the comfort travelling over indifferent surfaces, and the tyres of 3½-inch section are generous in proportion to the weight of the car...

'The body is one of the most successful we have seen on an Austin Seven. The wide, louvred, bonnet, reminiscent of the one used on the Ulster model, gives the car an appearance of solidity, and the long swept wings avoid the impression of dumpiness which one is liable to get on short wheelbase cars.'

Motor Sport's test revealed some of the differing attitudes of motorists in the 1930s, where those who had fully mastered 'crash' gearboxes had a tendency to despise synchromesh as being soppy, and still double-declutched as though it wasn't there ... and thought little of modifying the controls to suit their physique. It is also interesting to note that the tyres which seem so incredibly narrow today were considered quite wide fifty years ago. A very box-like body built by A.E. Wright with only one door, on the passenger side, also aroused little comment from *The Light Car*. They considered it quite normal, indeed quite attractive, when they tested it on a £135 model—based on a standard chassis—in August 1933:

'The main features are a lengthened bonnet, generous louvring of bonnet and valance, and the unusually capacious luggage boot—which will accommodate far more than the proverbial suitcase...

'As each car is individually built, customers' special requirements can be met, and Mr Wright makes a point of carrying out slight deviations from standard. Supertuning, for instance, can be undertaken, any colour scheme can be supplied (this without additional cost) and many extras, such as headlamp stoneguards and dummy hub caps can be provided as desired...'

The Light Car then went on to stage one of the first—if not the first—comparison test when they tried a de luxe saloon and a tourer back to back in July 1934, reporting:

'Comparisons are not always odious; in fact, they are at times very interesting. Particularly is this so when the two objects are similar in certain respects and yet, in other respects, are vastly different. The two seven horsepower models ... are basically similar, ... but the bodies fitted are entirely different styles. The type made little difference, both were

The Light Car carried one of the first comparison tests in 1934 between a tourer and a de luxe saloon.

attractive cars and both possessed the advantages of comfort, reliability and economy.

'Dealing first with the saloon model there is, of course, accommodation for two children or one adult in the rear seat. The actual measurements are:

'Inside the body across the rear seats the width is 42½ ins, while the measurement between the armrests is 35 ins. When the adjustable front seats are in the forward position, the measurement from the rear seat squab to the back of the front seats is 29½ ins.

'The range of adjustment of the front seats is 3½ ins and the distance from pedal pad to seatback may be varied from 38½ ins to 42 ins. As to headroom, there is nearly 37 ins above the driver's seat.

'Although only two doors are provided, they are really wide, so that, in conjunction with the tip-up front seats, they give easy access to the rear compartment.

'For all four passengers there are pneumatic seat cushions, and the upholstery is carried out in really good leather. In spite of the low price of the car, there is, in fact, nothing "cheap" about it.

'As evidence of this, several items of equipment may be mentioned. An interior visor is so mounted that when not required it folds up against the roof, but a touch of the finger brings it into position when required. All the glass, and not only the windscreen, is Triplex. A cover is provided for the spare wheel.

'A feature which particularly appealed to everyone who rode in the car was the floor covering. This consists of tough rubber shaped to fit nicely over the propeller shaft tunnel. Evidently it will remain in good condition longer than any carpet, and its smooth surface is very much easier to keep clean . . .

'Mention must also be made of the remarkably easy change gear. This applies just as much to second as to third and top, which have synchromesh mechanism.

'Another point is the lightness of the steering, which quality is not in this case obtained by means of a low steering ratio. Actually, from full lock to full lock, the wheel makes only one and one third turns, so that manoeuvring in a restricted space is simplicity itself.

'Turning to the other model tested, the two-seater, this proved to be a most attractive little motor car. So far as body space is concerned there was really ample room in the two bucket seats for the largest driver and passenger. In addition, the space inside the tail could be used for carrying luggage and was sufficient to hold two really good-sized suitcases.

'The all-weather equipment was efficient, consisting of two side curtains arranged so that they could be folded back from the centre and a hood which was simple both to erect and put down again.

'The design of the chassis is, of course, similar to that of the saloon and the performance was, if anything, a trifle better, owing, of course, to the lighter weight. For example, although the maximum speed over the quarter mile was 50.3 mph (slightly lower than the saloon, which achieved 51.7 mph), the average worked out at 47.66 mph (against 46.2 mph) while the standing quarter mile was covered in 31 seconds (against 31.6 seconds).

'Knowing that the Austin Seven has always been a tenacious little climber, it was decided to try the 1934 two-seater on one or two of the steeper hills in Surrey, with results that were definitely surprising. The first hill attempted was Bagden, on the road between Burford Bridge and Great Bookham. This has two severe bends and a maximum gradient of 1 in 1¾ and, owing to the narrowness of the road, it is impossible to get a run at it. Nevertheless, the Austin surmounted the crest at 14 mph in second gear.

'Whitedowns Hill, which was regarded in the past as a test hill, was treated in the same cavalier fashion and Pebblecombe Hill, on the Betchworth-Tadworth road, was taken almost joyously in second gear.

'Finding that hills of this type presented no difficulties, it was decided to try something considerably stiffer. The goat track up the side of Boxhill was attempted and, although it has a surface consisting almost entirely of very large bumps and very deep potholes, the car made a good climb.

'Finally, in an effort to find a hill that would really make the gallant little engine work hard, Westcott, which leads from Westcott village to Ranmore Common—and which is used in present-day motorcycle trials—was approached.

'In this instance, although bottom gear was needed and the engine was extended almost to its full capacity, there was never a moment of doubt as to whether the summit would be reached or not. The maximum gradient of this hill is in the neighbourhood of 1 in 4 and its average gradient for about half a mile is 1 in 5¼.'

Many modern cars can climb such gradients, but there are few which cope with surfaces at the same time like that of the goat track... *The Light Car* also harped back to this historic test when next they tried an Austin Seven, a Ruby saloon in December 1934. They reminisced:

'Taking, in the first place, the consideration of roominess, it will not perhaps be out of place to quote a passage from our commentary on the 1934 model: "There is ... accommodation for two children or one adult in the rear seat." During the great part of the present test the rear seats were occupied by two adults, quite of average size. Both volunteered a high opinion of the comfort in which they rode: neither experienced a suspicion of cramping. The width of the rear compartment between armrests is 35 ins. Above the rests the dimension is 43½ ins. The headroom available is sufficient for the tallest driver, the distance from rear seat to roof being 32 ins.

'The sliding roof and the hinged rear quarter windows—a new feature, the latter—provide the means of adequate ventilation; indeed, the occupants of the Ruby saloon need at no time suffer martyrdom to that

The occupants of the Ruby saloon need at no time suffer martyrdom to the musty closeness of atmosphere which is sometimes associated with small cars, quoth *The Light Car* in 1934.

musty closeness of atmosphere which is sometimes associated with small cars.

'The visibility afforded in the Austin is really exceptional, owing to the narrowness of the roof pillars and the sensibly erect seating positions. The use of real leather for the pneumatic upholstery lends something of "expensiveness" to the interior of this inexpensive little car.

'The ample width of the two doors makes ingress to and egress from the rear seats a comparatively easy matter even for portly or aged passengers; and with the adjustable front seats set in their farthest-back position there is a full 7½ ins of knee room for the back seat occupants.

'The ability of Seven owners to worm a dexterous path through traffic-thronged streets has long been a by-word. In this respect, the latest saloon is well up to its forbears. Three factors go to make this so: the little-restricted view of his surroundings which the driver enjoys, the responsive and quite high-geared steering (1¼ turns from lock to lock) and the capacity of the engine to pick up smartly at the lower end of its speed range. The man at the wheel does not—indeed, cannot—lounge; and his erectness somehow gives him the extra alertness which counts for so much nowadays...'

So you took your medicine as dispensed by Sir Herbert Austin and liked it ... although *The Light Car* fell back into a hint of criticism when they allowed the Ruby to run fast:

'The rubber buffers on which the engine is mounted do their work well, and all but a mere tremor of vibration is absorbed. On falling gradients, the Seven could, no doubt, be persuaded to reach 55 mph or so, although some vibration might be expected at that speed. With one passenger the car cruises comfortably at 35–38 mph; carrying a full load it is happiest between 33 mph and 35 mph. The slowest pulling speed on even load in top gear is about 9 mph. And the maximum was 48.91 mph, timed by a stopwatch. The mean speed over opposite directions on a flying quarter mile was 46.39 mph with a standing quarter mile covered in 31.4 seconds. Fuel consumption was 45 mpg ... and tests were becoming ever more scientific.'

Evidence that road tests were becoming ever more scientific was revealed when it was stated that the maximum speed, one-way, was 48.9 mph—timed by a stopwatch. The mean average speed, two-ways over a flying quarter mile, was 46.3 mph and the standing quarter mile covered in 31.4 seconds. Fuel consumption worked out at 45 mpg.

But there was still room for more adulation:

'A word of very definite praise is due to the rear luggage carrier—one of the neatest things of its kind yet seen. Adequately strong for all normal loads, it is yet sufficiently compact to stow away inside the spare wheel compartment when not in use. This leaves the tail of the body entirely free from excresence. The whole rear part of the car is, in fact, a little work of art.'

The Autocar were happy to emphasise how well the Ruby bustled on its way when they tested one in March 1935, adding little, however, to *The Light Car*'s eloquence—just a few extra miles per hour: 50.85 in one direction, 50.14 average, although they had to admit that the climb from 45 mph was slow. But all that was cleared up when next they tested a Ruby with the three-bearing engine in November 1936:

'With a car such as this the sheer performance aspect, as shown by the figures on paper, matters very little indeed, for its whole object and purpose are achieved if it provides reliable and safe transport for a number of people from the driver alone up to four at need. There is no question but that the Austin Seven fulfills these requirements. It has a name for trustworthiness that many another car might envy, its economy of operation is proverbial, and, as all kinds of tests at different times have demonstrated, it is capable of going almost anywhere four wheels can travel. Although,

The Ruby saloon had a name for trustworthiness that many a car might envy . . . and proved capable of going almost anywhere four wheels could travel, said *The Autocar* in 1935.

then, the actual performance is of secondary importance, as has just been remarked, it is none the less a point to bring out that the latest Seven is measurably superior to its predecessors on all counts. Its acceleration is better, it can hold on longer to top gear on the level, it will keep up its 40 mph or so more easily, and it has a distinctly higher maximum speed in reserve as compared to its forerunners.

'One significant point in this direction is that whereas when the Austin Seven was last tested in this fashion by *The Autocar* it was not possible to record acceleration figures involving 50 mph, which was virtually the full maximum speed of the car in favourable conditions, this latest model has been able to maintain almost 53 mph against the stop watch. The speedometer, incidentally, then showed a highest reading of 59–60. As to the lower speeds, the instrument was 3.1 mph fast at 30, and 4 mph fast at 40.'

There were other points about the new Ruby which *The Autocar* appreciated:

'Much can be done, of course, by using the gears on occasion, especially as they are quiet, and quickly and surely engaged. A driver who recognises the value of indirect gears on a small car can obtain a great deal more from the Seven than one who changes down as a last resort. It would seem that no appreciably great travel has been given to the clutch pedal ... but the new clutch, with a spring centre, is definitely smoother in taking up the drive, and that without special care being exercised.

'The new brakes are of Girling type, and they give confidence. A satisfactory emergency stop can be achieved without "standing" on the pedal, and ordinary slowing down for traffic needs is obtained with a light and easy application.'

The Motor also tested a Ruby in the same week, recording a 55 mph top speed, with a 28-second standing quarter mile, before a new magazine, *Practical Motorist*, achieved even more: 58 mph, timed by a Longines' (Baume and Co) split-second chronometer, which they proudly announced was 'one of the most accurate instruments available.' Acceleration figures obtained with the help of this formidable device included 11.4 seconds for the 0–30 mph and 58 seconds to reach top speed from rest. A Ferodo-Tapley meter was employed to test braking efficiency, which worked out at 81 per cent on dry concrete, with a 37-ft stopping distance from 30 mph. *Practical Motorist* said:

'However hard the brakes were applied there was no tendency for the car to swerve or skid on a dry road; when this was repeated on a greasy road the car slid forward in a straight line—proof of the accurate automatic compensation provided by the Girling system.'

So much for cadence braking ... but cars were driven a good deal more sedately in those days. *The Light Car* found a pre-production version of the Big Seven to be distinctly lively on the road in a brief test in July 1937, however:

'According to the speedometer, the Big Seven does 62 mph on the level. As a check on that figure, it is interesting to record that on a slight main road gradient the speed was 58 mph up hill and 66 mph down hill.

'On what might be described roughly as typical main road gradients in the Midlands, it appeared that this car was always capable of 50 mph and usually could touch a bit more. Its acceleration at low speeds and even in the higher ranges was distinctly good.

'This is perhaps best shown by the "all round" figure of the time required to accelerate from a standstill to 50 mph. The Big Seven did it in 26 seconds and for the benefit of those who have nothing with which to compare this, it may be stated without fear of contradiction that this result is definitely good for a car of this general size and type.

'Taking what may be a more useful figure for many people, we tested the Big Seven from 10 mph to 30 mph using second and third gears, which ratios would presumably be used by anybody who was in a hurry to accelerate from this low speed. The result in this case was 7 seconds, again a very good figure.'

Road tests would never be the same again with the introduction of more and more traffic lights making the 0–50 mph, and eventually, 0–60 mph times of ever-increasing importance. *The Motor*'s road test of the Big Seven saloon the next month had a far more modern ring to it with a fair element of criticism and more comprehensive performance figures: 56.25 mph maximum for the flying quarter mile, 42 mph in third gear and 26.5 mph in second; an 8-second 10–30 mph time in third gear; a 16-second 10–30 mph in top; a 23-second 30–50 mph in top; a 25.4-second 0–50 mph using all the gears and a 9-second 0–30 with a 25.4-second standing start quarter mile. It was calculated that the Big Seven could climb a 1-in-3.9 hill in bottom gear and cover 32 mpg, driven hard. And using the brake pedal only, it was possible to stop from 30 mph in 41 ft and from 50 mph in 120. Motorists were demanding more and more data ... but *The Motor* did not let them down when it came to description and comment either:

'The Austin Big Seven saloon definitely meets the demand for a four-door edition of the popular and ubiquitous "Seven", having withal a brisk performance. It gives uncramped four-seater accommodation with fairly wide doors, allowing easy entry and egress, and the six lights ensure a good all-round standard of visibility. True to Austin style, the windows are deep, the headroom is almost lavish for the front-seat occupants, being appreciably better than is found in many a larger car, and sufficient at the rear.

'The model tested was equipped with a sliding roof which gives a wide opening, sliding back some 20 ins. The front seats are upholstered with "Float-on-Air" pneumatic cushions, comfortable and conforming to the body contour; the squabs fit round one's back but are on the hard side. The front seats are of the chair style, so that one sits upright, but while this may not be so pleasing for the passenger, it is perfectly satisfactory for the driver, placing him in an excellent position for the control of the car ...

'On the open road the Austin Big Seven settles down to cruising at 45 mph without the engine becoming audible. In town, when within the 30 mph limit, it motors quietly and easily, having withal sufficient low-speed torque to allow the majority of town work to be covered on top and third speeds. For the lazy driver, it will pull away from a crawl without great torque reaction and vibration, but, naturally, it is better to change to second.

'The clutch is of an improved design; there is a fair travel for the pedal and no delicate control is demanded to ensure smooth take-up; both on the getaway and when changing it engages sweetly.

'The gearbox calls for commendation. The synchromesh works well, so that no especial skill or timing is demanded to make positively silent and quick changes. This facility encourages the driver, no doubt, to make liberal use of the box. Added to this, the pinions run quietly, being of the helical constant-mesh type.

'As opposed to these good features, it behoves us to criticise the transmission from the gearbox rearwards, for it cannot be classed as smooth, the final drive whining slightly under load and "grumbling" audibly on the overrun from cruising speeds.

'The steering is, needless to say, very light and easily controlled but is not possessed of a very strong self-centring action, so that the car has to be steered the whole time.

'Braking is smooth, pulling the car up dead square and giving stopping figures in the region of 70 per cent [efficiency] . . .

'The springing is one of the best features of the new model; the lengthened wheelbase and wider track combined with the use of extra low pressure tyres of 4.75 ins section, have given a new standard of riding comfort and stability to the Austin Seven. It will travel safely and without the terrific buffeting and pitching that might be expected over roads in almost unmade condition.'

The Autocar also pleaded for more self-centring action in the steering during a similar road test in October 1937, before *The Light Car* got to grips with a Big Seven again in January 1938. They did not record so much data as *The Motor* but went to a lot of trouble to describe what it was like to sit behind the wheel of a Big Seven, especially if the reader was a "Baby Seven" owner and thinking of changing up:

'Despite an all-round enlargement, the Big Seven has very much the same "feel" as the Baby Seven, but it is fair to say that the larger car is rather better in almost every respect. It is faster and more lively. Its brakes are more effective and, unexpectedly, it has an even smaller turning circle.

'Probably the principal advantage which the Big Seven has over its smaller counterpart is in the matter of body space. The car has four doors, which are hinged at their outer edges and close on to the centre pillars. The front doors are 25 ins wide and the rear ones measure 21½ ins so that access is easy either to the front or to the rear seats.

'Inside the body there is a width of 42 ins across both sets of seats and the rear cushion is 36½ ins wide between the armrests. Naturally, both front seats are adjustable, the range of movement being 5½ ins. Leg room for the driver can thus be varied from 37½ ins up to 43 ins. In the rear compartment the seat cushion measures 18½ ins from back to front and the knee space is 4½ ins to 10 ins, according to the position of the front seats.

'Headroom is always important. At the back of this Austin it measures 35½ ins and above the front seats it is 40 ins. Another dimension which has much to do with the driver's comfort is the height of his seat above the floor. In the Big Seven the effective height is about 11 ins, although the front edge of the seat is considerably higher, so that it supports the thighs admirably.

'All this probably accounts in part for the fact that the car is not at all tiring to drive, even on long journeys. That result is also due, no doubt, to the excellent support which the squab gives to the driver's back. Still another factor probably is the comfortable position of the steering wheel, low in the driver's lap. A man of medium height can see the bottom edge of the windscreen over the rim of the steering wheel.

'From some of these facts it may be deduced that there is a good field of view forward. That is so. The road surface can be seen as close as 10 ft ahead and the near-side wing lamp also is visible from the driving seat. Equally good is the visibility rearwards. Thanks to a comparatively high back window, the driving mirror gives a view not merely of 30 yds, or 40 yds backward along a level road, but to infinity if that somewhat theoretical term is permissible.'

You could almost hear the salesman talking . . .

The Practical Motorist, equipped with their comprehensive instruments, discovered that the Forlite saloon was, as was to be expected, a little bit quicker than the Sixlite, when they tested one in July 1938. They reported:

'Performance was much better than expected, and . . . as an example of this, the time required to reach 30 mph from a standstill, using first, second and third gears, was 8.6 seconds; using second and third only the time was just 9 seconds. From 10 to 30 mph took 7 seconds when using second and third gears, and 8.4 seconds when using third gear only. Acceleration from 20 to 40 mph required 10.2 seconds in third gear, or 14.8 seconds in top. From 30 to 50 mph in top required 19.8 seconds. From a standstill we were able to reach 50 mph in 26.6 seconds . . .

'At first one was inclined to feel that the car was rather unsteady compared with others, most of which are larger, but any qualms in this direction were quickly thrown off after driving for a few miles. The car proved to be unusually steady considering the short wheelbase, and it held the road particularly well when cornering fairly quickly or when swerving to overtake. Steering, too, was very good and accurate although slightly heavy when approaching full lock.'

The Motor managed to extract the magic 60 mph from a Forlite, with similar acceleration times to *Practical Motorist*, during a test in August 1938 before going on to say:

'Outstanding because of its particular design is the steering, which is practically devoid of self-centring action. To the man who drives a variety of cars this system is at first disconcerting, but within 100 miles or so suspicion as to the probable behaviour of the front wheels disappears completely and one is left with the full realisation that the Big Seven can be placed most accurately with the absolute minimum of effort.

'In several other ways the car grows more and more likeable as the miles go by. The suspension feels on the soft side when driving at 50 mph along a main road. Turn off the highway on to an unmade series of potholes and the result is an absolute revelation. The Big Seven simply delights in cart tracks and passenger shock insulation is so good that there is every temptation to depart from the beaten track for the sheer enjoyment of the process.

'The greater part of one day was devoted to sampling the behaviour of the car in London traffic. Despite the aforementioned suitability for rough country conditions, the Austin Big Seven is singularly successful in heavy traffic. Acceleration up to 40 mph is really brisk and it is only thereafter that the power curve begins to flatten out. Consequently both for congested areas and much-used by-passes the car excels on account of its extreme handiness and rapid getaway.

'On wet tramlines the general stability was found to be of a high order while the Girling brakes gave a smooth deceleration calculated to inspire confidence under such conditions. The available lock enabled the car to be turned right round in confined surroundings such as the Edgware Road, and it is noteworthy that only two turns sufficed to swing the steering wheel from lock to lock...

'Body arrangements are such as to suggest that an enthusiastic owner-driver is responsible for the layout.

'The Austin Big Seven is one of the easiest cars to enter we have ever encountered. The new running boards assist the elderly without impeding the active. From the driving seat most people will step straight onto the road. Incidentally, these running boards keep the coachwork remarkably clean and thus serve a dual purpose.

'The large cubby hole to the left of the facia board has a downward slope of about 45 degrees and thus sets an example which all designers will be well advised to follow. No matter how steep the hill or how violent the acceleration, everything in this cavity remains in position and a potential source of infuriation is thereby eliminated. Beneath the tip up front seats are two confined but useful areas wherein cameras and the like may be stored out of harm's way...

'It is difficult to imagine a more soundly and sensibly designed motorcar to be obtained at anything like the price.'

A sad note crept into the last test—by *The Light Car*—of an Austin Seven when it was new. They were unable to record the maximum speed of their Sixlite Saloon in January 1939 because 'Brooklands track was in a state of disrepair—sadly resembling a Spanish battlefront...' It had been on that hallowed track that the Austin Seven had made its name in competition with exploits covered in the next chapter.

VII
The Austin Seven in Competition

The excellent reactions of the specialist motoring press once they had tried an Austin Seven encouraged the company to participate in motor sport—provided not too much money was needed. Austin was still struggling when the Seven was introduced and even by the 1920s it was readily apparent how much money could be wasted on motor sport. In subsequent years, a great deal of time was spent on Austin Seven racing development, but only when the company could afford it. In the meantime, the stark simplicity of the car and wondrous way in which parts could be swopped around fostered the efforts of impecunious enthusiasts in all spheres of motor sport. Some of the most ingenious specials ever built were based on the Austin Seven.

It has been said with conviction that there is nothing in which a motor manufacturer is less interested than the model it has just stopped making—so it was hardly surprising that Austin did not continue with works Sevens after the war. It had far more to occupy its development engineers. But the enormous number of Austin Sevens that survived the hostilities continued to fascinate special builders. Some of the greatest competition car designers, notably Colin Chapman of Lotus, cut their teeth on Austin Seven specials. Eventually supplies of spare parts dwindled and the club they all supported, the 750MC, had to encourage alternative development; but it still continues today with Austin Sevens in more historic guise.

Although the first success in competition has been recorded as being by company tester Lou Kings, with one of the Austin Seven prototypes, which climbed Shelsley Walsh in 89.8 seconds in July 1922, the story does not really begin until 1923; the factory had enough on its hands getting the first cars into production.

But Sir Herbert's son-in-law, Capt. Arthur Waite, was itching to show what the Austin Seven could achieve. He managed to get a car stripped of everything that was not strictly necessary for the road so that it could run with a higher 4.5:1 rear axle ratio—and promptly lapped Brooklands at 62.64 mph to beat the cycle-car opposition against which it competed on Easter Monday 1923. Having demonstrated that the car would not make a fool of itself, he then took it to Monza for the Italian Cycle Car Grand Prix and won the 750-cc class, again with a fastest lap of 64 mph. This feat aroused great interest as the first British victory in Continental Europe since the First World War—and was appealing to Austin because it was so far away that it would not have attracted much attention had the car lost!

Sir Herbert must have been feeling quite good about racing when he was approached soon after by a motor trader, Gordon England, to build a similar car to Waite's for competition in Britain. In more highly-tuned form, the two cars lapped Brooklands at more than 70 mph, with two further cars being prepared for Kings and H. Cutler:

The Waite, Cutler and Kings cars were then taken to Boulogne for an important light-car race as a works team. The performance had been further

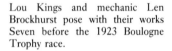

Lou Kings and mechanic Len Brockhurst pose with their works Seven before the 1923 Boulogne Trophy race.

improved by fitting them with twin Cox-Atmos carburettors, a triple-branch exhaust and high-lift camshaft that enabled them to run at 5000 rpm. It was their undoing and highlighted the lubrication problem that was subsequently combatted by the special crankshaft tubing.

Gordon England, meanwhile, continued to develop his racer with some measure of independence, leaving the impression that Sir Herbert was backing both horses—a works team and a capable amateur who might bring Austin a lot of good publicity if he won but could be disowned if he lost. The engine of Gordon England's car was even more highly tuned with a higher compression cylinder head and forced-feed lubrication, the overall weight having been brought down to 840 lb with a single-seater body. In this form it broke several records at Brooklands at speeds up to 79.62 mph for five miles and 64.7 mph for

100 miles. An ultra-lightweight two-seater body, weighing only 20 lb, was then fitted for the Brooklands 200-mile race in October. This car, with Gordon England at the wheel, proved capable of lapping consistently at 79 mph to split a team of works French Salmsons and take a highly-popular second place in the 1100-cc class despite its capacity of only 747 cc.

It was from these two basic forms of competition car that the Sports and Brooklands Super-Sports models were developed. Waite continued to develop the works cars as Gordon England sold his versions to customers; both efforts met with a lot of success before they collided head-on, as it were, in the Brooklands 200-mile race of 1924. A new 750-cc class had been instigated and turned out to be an Austin Seven preserve. The rate of attrition was high before Gordon England ran out a lucky winner at 75.61 mph—with plumes of smoke three laps from the end heralding a broken connecting rod and piston. Lubrication problems had eliminated most of the other runners in the 750-cc class as lap speed rose to 80 mph. In general, Gordon England seemed to win most of the races that mattered that year, including one at the inaugural meeting of the new Montlhery track near Paris. It was a happy hunting ground for England, for he set most of the year's records there in October, varying from 300 miles at 80 mph to a fastest lap at 84.10 mph. He also managed to annex every Brooklands class record from half a mile to 200!

Waite realised that it would need dramatic technical changes to be sure of beating Gordon England, so he looked to supercharging, which had liberated a lot more power for Peugeot. By using a Roots-type triple-impeller supercharger, he discovered that he could raise the power of a side-valve Austin Seven engine from 25 bhp to 43 bhp—one more than the twin-overhead-camshaft 746-cc Peugeot had achieved. The Austin's compression ratio had to be lowered to 4.8:1, however, to keep the cylinder head on the block at 5 psi! The chassis was also lowered with underslung springs and a canted radiator used for better air penetration that saw his experimental car reach 88 mph early in 1925. Following various teething problems, an even lighter fabric body was fitted to the single-seater in time to take a two-way flying-start mile record at 84.29 mph with a one-way best of 92.44 mph at Brooklands. But everything was not rosy: the magical 100 mph needed to justify the very heavy expenditure in supercharging still seemed a long way off because far less extensively-modified cars were capable of more than 80 mph.

Waite also had a second supercharged car bored out to 775 cc to run in 1100 cc racing, with both machines enjoying a reasonable amount of success. George Duller even managed to win one race in the 775-cc car at an astounding 89.9 mph, although it was Gordon England again who outlasted everybody to win the 750-cc class in the Brooklands 200-mile race!

Gordon England then decided to retire from racing, leaving private entrants such as Francis Samuelson to enter events in his cars, along with Waite and others, such as C.V.M. Walther, who used a Boyd-Carpenter Seven. Interest was waning in the 750-cc class of the Brooklands 200-mile race, however, and England was persuaded to make a comeback to provide sufficient

numbers for the class to continue in the 1926 event. Incredibly, it provided his third successive class win as most of his rivals succumbed to various ailments, although Waite ran well in the 1100-cc class until his car's body collapsed. He had the consolation of holding 13 international records, however, before emigrating to Australia to run the local Austin distributorship. Samuelson also took fourth place in the 1100-cc class at Boulogne, and Zubiaga third in the same class in the Targa Florio, which did Austin's publicity no harm at all.

Once Waite and Gordon England were out of the way, private owners saw better opportunities for success with their Austin Sevens, although the 200-mile race still presented a problem in that it was really too tough for anything other than top-flight machinery. The cars that had been raced by Waite and Gordon England were attractive, naturally. Waite's supercharged record-breaker— minus engine—was sold to be raced as 'Slippery Ann' by a gentleman called Coldicutt; Gordon England's 200-mile racer was bought by Boyd-Carpenter, who also took over the Gordon England tuning enterprise.

'Slippery Ann'—pictured in 1926—
became one of the most successful
early Austin Seven racers.

This arrangement suited Gordon England well because he wanted to concentrate on producing saloon cars, and he could still take advantage of the publicity that their exploits generated. Soon after, Boyd-Carpenter, with fellow director C.K. Chase, took a modified Cup model called Mr Jo Jo to a series of long-distance records at Brooklands. They captured everything from three hours to twelve hours at between 62 and 63 mph, such was their consistency, and their success was all the more satisfying because they took the records from Peugeot. To complete their score, Chase went on to help take the only one left, the 24-hour, at Montlhery! Meanwhile, the original Gordon England 200-mile race car was retained as Mrs Jo Jo...

Amazingly, in the hands of H.C. Spero, this gallant old car outlasted all the latest Austin Seven specials to win its class and take eighth place overall in the Brooklands 200-mile race of 1928!

Austin Sevens also continued to be successful in short races because so many were run to handicaps. Waite, also, had not lost his competitive instinct, using an Austin Seven to win the first Australian Grand Prix over 100 miles in 1928.

Back in Britain, the lack of an alternative to Brooklands was being keenly felt. Various attempts had been made to simulate a road circuit within the confines of the historic banked track, but essentially races there remained just a flat-out blind; and the body governing British motor sport, the RAC, could not hold Continental-style road races elsewhere on the mainland because such activities were banned on public highways. There was a strong element of thought, supported notably by Sir Herbert Austin, that the best publicity and technological development was to be gained from cars bearing a close resemblance to normal production machines rather than racing machines built purely for storming around a banked track, and preferably on normal roads. So the RAC decided to return to Northern Ireland, where roads could be closed for racing, and the great Gordon Bennett races had been held before the First World War.

The first of their new races coincided with the advent of the Austin Seven's first real competitor, the Morris Minor, in 1928. Sporting success obviously helped to sell cars, so it was with great interest that Sir Herbert Austin watched the Ulster Grand Prix, especially as he had just introduced his new Super Sports model. Austin were represented, unofficially, by the brothers J.D. and F.S. Barnes, their car having a five-lap start to cover 341 miles against the bigger cars' maximum of 410 miles. They led for five laps before falling back because they were too slow. Slippery Ann, in the hands of Coldicutt, had also beaten two of the Super Sports prototypes at the Shelsley Walsh hill climb, so Sir Herbert had plenty to think about as 1929 approached.

The economic depression was already beginning to strike motor racing, but although the number of events at Brooklands was reduced, they included the next best thing to the Le Mans 24-hour race! This new event had to be split into two 12-hour races, from 8 am to 8 pm on consecutive days, because of objections by residents living near the track to the noise of the cars. It was left to the Barnes brothers' car, painted orange like the works machines, to uphold Austin's honour, which they did with great panache, especially as they were the only entrant in their class. With no opposition to worry about, they kept their average speed down to 49 mph and completed the course without incident—and then received a massive 55-lap start in a six-hour race that followed six weeks later! In this case they speeded up to more than 50 mph, and running with great regularity, nearly won the event!

The sporting Gunnar Poppe, who had thoroughly enjoyed himself with one of the prototype Super Sports at Shelsley Walsh, then decided to go motor

Gunnar Poppe at the wheel of his 1929 competition car with a backing group which includes Alf Depper and expert manager J. Shepherd.

racing as a relaxation from captaining the London Welsh rugby team. In his first big race, the Irish Grand Prix at Phoenix Park, Dublin, he proved outstandingly fast, but only just managed to secure a place for his Super Sports when he ran out of petrol through inexperience.

The rest of the Austin team did not do particularly well either, so Sir Herbert decided that he needed an experienced team manager if they were to be a success in Britain's oldest road race, the Tourist Trophy, in Ulster later that year. Waite was still in Australia, so he asked Gordon England. England was happy to oblige, but demanded full control above even Sir Herbert, of what had

All ready for action, just waiting for its number ... one of the 1930 Tourist Trophy Austin Sevens.

become a rather disconsolate team. Despite Austin's protests, he got it and needed all this authority to pull them into shape.

Poppe did not compete in the TT, but his partner at Shelsley Walsh, S.V. Holbrook, son of Austin's sales manager, proved just as fast, along with the experienced Archie Frazer Nash. A massive crowd was thrilled to see the tiny Austins hang on grimly as Rudolph Caracciola in his works Mercedes could only slowly pare away their five-lap start. Campari also caught them in an Alfa Romeo, but the Austins did so well their name was on everybody's lips. Frazer Nash's third place and Holbrook's fourth had ensured that the supercharged sports Austin would subsequently be known as the Ulster. It needed only a sixth place overall for Holbrook in the Brooklands 500-mile race later in the season to make 1929 a year of triumph for the Ulsters.

The 1930 Brooklands 500-mile single-seater not only had special bodywork, but Dunlop Cord racing tyres that closely followed the lines of world record-breaking rubberware.

The following year was made a good deal tougher by the emergence of the new M.G. Midget with its more advanced overhead camshaft engine and four-speed gearbox, although Austin's racing effort was reinforced by the return of Waite from Australia. The main effort was concentrated on the supercharged Ulster although normally-aspirated versions continued to be entered to take maximum advantage of handicapping. Frazer Nash had distributor problems with the leading supercharged Austin Seven in the Brooklands Double 12-hour race, and although Waite was seventh overall, and Barnes tenth in a non-supercharged car, M.G.s took the prestigious team prize with 14th, 18th and 19th places overall. Waite then switched to an unblown car for the Irish Grand Prix and was promptly tipped as favourite to win—but Victor Gillow took first place in a Riley. Waite's disappointment was compounded by officials flagging him in a lap early and then displacing him from second to fifth position when they discovered their mistake. Sir Herbert was furious and threatened to quit racing, but could not because it would have seemed that they were afraid of the M.G. menace. In any case, the team had already entered the Ulster TT, with Waite, Frazer Nash and Poppe as drivers. Waite crashed, Frazer Nash had engine trouble, and Poppe hung on to take fifth place behind a trio of the all-conquering Alfa Romeos and a big Alvis, so Austin were not disgraced.

Classic of classics ... the 1930 Ulster as it stands today.

Waite was still recovering from a broken jaw when Bentley star Sammy Davis took his seat in the Brooklands 500-mile race, which had become a classic

such was the pace and the excitement of the previous year's event. A good insight into the intense, yet sporting, competition in these events and the whole era of the 1920s and 1930s was given by journalist Davis, in his last article, in 1981, for the British magazine *Collector's Car* (now *Sporting Cars*). He wrote:

'Driving a small car in a long race is every bit as exciting as driving a large one. It's true you don't get the magnificent feeling of a large machine going very fast, fitting into the popular idea of racing, always plenty of excitement and a thunderous exhaust. But on the other hand, the small car is as lively as a small terrier, and at its most exciting when racing against larger machines.

'Our cars, painted a brilliant orange, had been used earlier in the Tourist Trophy and were now racing with most of the unwanted gear stripped from them. The 500-mile race, like nearly all of the long-distance events of those days, was run on a handicap. But it had its complications. If you were driving a small car, Pit Control had a headache in trying to relate the performance of their team cars against the performance of much larger cars. In this particular case we had the smallest cars in the race with an ambition of running the cars at an average speed faster than they had ever run before, and certainly faster than any other cars in the 750-cc class.

'First acquaintance with the machines showed that they were very lively. They had a feeling of absolute reliability and stability, which was unusual with racing cars as a rule...

'I had a partner on whom I could rely completely. He was, at that time, the Earl of March (later the Duke of Richmond and Gordon), and he had a good sense of humour, which is of the utmost importance in any team. He would do exactly what the signals told him, and could, of course, handle the car without any difficulty at all at any speed it would like to go. Lord Howe was driving in the same race on a bigger car, and that got a rather left-wing type of newspaper thoroughly worried, being really rude in a nice sort of way. It revealed that two Earls and 33 Misters had a race at Brooklands on a certain day. It didn't worry us in the least and was the subject of humour with all the other drivers.

'The handicap system consisted of giving the cars different lengths of race, that is to say that you would do fewer laps with a 750 than you would with a six litre. It was a plain track race, using the old outer circuit of Brooklands with no corner worth talking about from a technical point of view, only a very awkward bend between one banked curve, and another near the Vicker's shed. It should have been easy, but it was beginning to be tricky since it was essential to get on to the home banking exactly in the right place or trouble would come...

'On the day of the race, it rained. And there was quite a lot of unpleasantness at Brooklands on a wet track. However, it gave our Control quite a lot of pleasure, because we knew our cars were fast; we knew therefore, that the big cars would have to go for all they were worth, and rain is not the best thing when you are travelling at over 100 mph on the banking or anywhere else.

'My first spell was interesting because once again I felt that the car itself was absolutely right. It felt good, responded well to any request from the throttle, and it really was going quite fast. I don't know how fast because you only have a rev counter, not a speedometer; you had simply to guess the speed and wait until some scientist at Control could say what so many revs meant in miles per hour.

'Another thing that was good was that I knew many of the drivers of the other teams well. One knew that they could be relied upon to handle the car in very difficult circumstances, and you had to match this with tricks of your own. For instance, the people we knew for certain would be our chief opponents were the Bentleys, the Delage, and the Sunbeams. So whenever one of those came past you tucked in behind, thereby getting a considerable increase in speed owing to the slipstream. That had to be watched, of course, because if you stayed there too long the radiator didn't get enough air through it and one might have boiling trouble.

'But you could manage to get a lot of advantage from another fast car, even if its driver who knew quite well you were there did his best to take a line which should be more difficult for you. March took on for his spell and I was able to stroll about and have a talk with Control and we found that, broadly speaking, and if no accident or trouble occurred, we were very well placed indeed. In fact, we were somewhere about third to fourth most of the time, with the car having something in hand. On the other hand, two cars in the team had trouble quite early. One's engine trouble was serious, and that is always nasty because you don't know what is going to happen to your own.

'However, March kept the average exactly as he was told, and then I had my second spell. By that time, things had happened. Quite a number of cars had got into trouble because this is a very fast race, and the track was more or less strewn with people in distress and bits of the cars they had been driving.

'One bit was quite alarming. As I was going down the railway straight, that is the only long straight the track has, a wheel with its driving shaft came across my bows and began to do the most extraordinary gyrations making one wonder how the big cars were going to miss it. It was difficult enough for the small ones!

'The result was, of course, chaos for the very fast cars, but they all managed to get round. Having large chunks of metal and wheels of that sort as a handicap was not too good. As the withdrawals from trouble increased, our position became better and better until before the last hour of the race when we were actually leading, on handicap of course, with one of the Bentleys, a blower car driven by my old friend, Dr Benjafield, as our principal antagonist. Benji was certainly going, the sight of his car when it came past had all the glamour you get from the traditional racing car. A terrific amount of noise and general suggestion that it was just being held. Well, that made me think it was about time we went a bit faster. At that exact moment the control signals allowed us to go faster, and the following hour was one of the best in all my time racing.

'Benji knew perfectly well that he had the Austin as his principal antagonist, and he drove magnificently and took advantage of everything he could think of to get the car going faster, and he was obviously pretty nearly all out most of the time, certainly averaging over 110.

'On the other hand, I did a good deal of increased speed by cutting the corners, although that sounds rather odd on a bank track, you can take a line which allows you to cut the corner and at the same time take advantage of going steeply down the very high banking instead of following it round.

'It is a little tricky but as long as you know your car you are all right, and also of course I tacked on to Benji whenever I could, but Benji did his level best to shake me off and we went on like that, really enjoying ourselves. I was beginning to wonder whether I could really match his speed. But then without any warning at all one of his tyres flew to pieces, and the air was absolutely thick with bits of rubber. Benji managed to control the car, which was sliding about badly and seemed to maintain some sort of speed on what amounted to a bare wheel. He had been hit on the right arm, which he had been holding on the side of the car, by pieces of rubber. Although he was in pain, it didn't make any difference to the speed he maintained. Well, there was nothing for it but to go a bit faster, use more revs and hope for the best, we were very close to the finish. It worked.

'Just when I thought we would never do it, the secretary of the club running the 500 appeared with an enormous chequered flag; we passed it and we had won.

'The speeds were rather amusing. The Austin had actually averaged just a little over 83 mph. You must admit that is pretty good for a car of the size. Benji, with E.R. Hall as his partner, had averaged 111 mph for 500 miles, which takes some doing. He deserved to win, but that doesn't matter very much. If one gets a bit of luck and wins oneself, you can't spend too much time feeling sorry for people who ought to have won.'

The immediate result of this great victory was that the car was required to take as many 750-cc class records as possible as back-up publicity for the forthcoming London Motor Show at which the new, larger, saloon was to be introduced, and to help boost sales of the production low-chassis sports models, which had begun earlier that year. Davis went on:

'The records in question included the one for 12 hours. That meant that the car would be running on the track (Brooklands) after dark. It could not run beyond a certain time because the residents of St George's Hill naturally objected to the noise. But it could do 12 hours. The problem was what to do about the lighting.

'In a rather rash moment, I suggested that the best way would be to use the method S.F. Edge adopted when he was able to do the 24-hour record at Brooklands. That is, line the proper path for the car with red storm lanterns, in such a way that if the car kept the lanterns on its left and close by it was following the right track. I thought if Edge could do it, I could do it.

'My partner in the record, Charles Goodacre, agreed. The first part of the run was extremely good. The car, of course, had been stripped as much as possible, and in order to limit the number of pit stops it had been fitted with another tank where the mechanic's seat would have been. The tank was on the floorboards of the cockpit, kept in position by steel straps each lined with some furry sort of material. It seemed quite satisfactory, but what I found when we got to the darkness was that it was all very well saying you could do this because Edge did it, but Edge had headlights on his car. We had no headlights at all. The result was that every instinct you had got warned me that driving into pitch darkness at well over 80 mph was dangerous!

'One knew that if one followed the lights it was not dangerous. It was a wearying experience and not altogether pleasant, because the car appeared to be doing well over 100 at least, whereas it was actually doing about 85, and everything was out of proportion.

'One got accustomed to it, and we continued taking records all the time. But then something happened, which I call my ghost story.

'As I was coming off the Byfleet banking along the unbanked curve towards the home banking, something quite soft came across my face, stayed there for a thousandth of a second maybe, and disappeared. It was a shaking experience. I kept thinking what in the name of heaven was that? If it was a bird, although there were no birds about at night, hitting it at 80 would have been a very unpleasant experience, whereas this thing was quite soft. It couldn't have been a sheet of old newspaper that happened to be lying on the track. That again would have been a nasty experience and it wouldn't have left one's face.

'One went on guessing, then a thought occurred. If the underworld, or ghost world, was going to take a hand in records ... it was time one thought hard what to do about it ... And just when I was calming down, the darn thing did it again. Once was bad, but if it was going to make a habit of it, one had better go and see what was happening. At the same time the engine began to run irregularly and finally cut off. As it did there was a strong smell of petrol ... I coasted into the pit, and there the ghost story became a plain simple mechanical fact. What had happened was that the steel straps around the auxiliary petrol tank had for some reason come loose.

'This released the long soft material lining from their grip. The lining happened to be secured to the floor of the cockpit. Long streamers of felt were waving in the air alongside me...

'We finished our run and were thoroughly pleased with ourselves, because the 12-hour run average was just over 81 mph and it would take a long time for somebody else to beat that.'

In the face of an increasing threat to their supremacy by the M.G. Midgets, Waite became even more determined to build the first 750-cc car to reach 100 mph. For that very purpose, Malcolm Campbell was despatched to Daytona Beach in January 1931 with a supercharged Single-seater Seven, as an aside from attempting the world land speed record in his own car, Bluebird. Campbell managed to extract 94.061 mph on a two-way run in the Seven (and 245 mph for a world record in Bluebird) before his arch rival, Capt. George Eyston, broke the magic 100 mph barrier a month later in an M.G. Midget. Waite hit back by designing a new single-seater supercharged Seven with a streamlined body that was the result of much wind tunnel testing at Vicker's. Davis was nominated as

The supercharged engine as used in Malcolm Campbell's 100 mph record-attempt car of 1931.

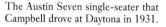

The Austin Seven single-seater that Campbell drove at Daytona in 1931.

The new streamlined supercharged Austin Seven used for the Brooklands Easter meeting in 1931 had a body based closely on Malcolm Campbell's world record breaking car, Bluebird.

the driver, but broke a leg in a crash with another car and his place was taken by that car's owner, Leon Cushman, as some form of recompense! It was an arrangement that worked well as Cushman eventually became the first driver to exceed 100 mph in a 750-cc car in Britain with the Austin.

By this time sufficient competition versions of the M.G. Midget had been built for them to outnumber as well as outclass Austin Sevens in blown and unblown forms in circuit racing. It should be mentioned, however, that they cost far more.

In only one major event, the Light Car Club's relay race at Brooklands, were the works Austin Sevens able to beat the M.G.s—and win a trophy donated by the M.G. Car Company, which had been confident of winning! This event was to become especially significant in Austin Seven history as the forerunner of the classic of British club racing, the Six-Hour Relay Race organised by the 750 Motor Club, which would be formed by Austin Seven owners in 1939.

The original relay race was devised because members of the Light Car Club—for machines under 1500 cc—were among the most avid supporters of the British national track, although few of them could afford to run in the glamorous long-distance races such as the Double Twelve. They did not even stand much change of finishing, such was the pace and the punishing nature of the circuit. This led the LCC to organise their relay for teams of three cars (of no more than 1500 cc capacity), each of which was scheduled to complete 30 laps, or 90 miles. Should any one car fail to finish its quota, the next in line could take over the sash which had to be carried to the end. And to give everybody a decent chance, the final result was run to a handicap.

Enthusiasm was immense at the start for this novel event. It represented a chance for the amateur to experience the thrills of long-distance racing, with pit work and all that entailed and the comradeship of a disciplined team. Ironically, the first race was won by the far-from-amateur works Austin Seven team, but they had to cope with such hazards as Morgan three-wheelers equipped with rubber bands. These held open their hand throttles so that the drivers were completely free to wrestle with the steering wheel as they ran round the rim of the banking!

Austin works involvement in competition continued in a lower key during 1932 as Eyston's 'Magic Midget' took most records worth having and it seemed unlikely that the side valve engine could be developed to produce a competitive amount of power. But there was consolation for Austin in the Earl of March beating two supercharged Midgets to win the 750-cc class of the British Empire Trophy race at more than 92 mph. The works team was unable to beat the Morgans in the LCC Relay race, however, because of more severe handicapping, and gave the TT, and a 1,000-mile race to replace the Double Twelve, a miss.

Enthusiastic amateurs continued to race Austin Sevens successfully in other events. A.N.L. Maclachlan bought a Gordon England Brooklands model that had been to America with the specific intent of giving Oxford a boost in the Inter-Varsity Speed Trials. Suitably stripped down, this car won the 1100-cc class before serving as his everyday transport and winning a gold medal in the 1928 London-to-Land's End Trial. Events such as these had been organised by the Motor Cycling Club since 1904 for a mixture of cars and motor cycles. They amounted to the forerunners of modern day rallying with competitors being required to complete a route of several hundred miles in around 24 hours. In the early days, cars' lights were crude and the roads were rough; it was a formidable task. Such tests soon attracted a lot of attention in the Press and were seen as good publicity if cars could complete them satisfactorily. As the cars got better, vicious and badly-surfaced hills were added to sort them out.

Interest reached such fever pitch by the mid-1920s that works teams were banned to keep down the costs, but winning a gold medal for clearing all the test hills without stopping and on schedule was still a mighty achievement. The sheer versatility of the Austin Seven was emphasised by the fact that Maclachlan could use it for such events and then continue a racing career...

Subsequently the car still proved capable of lapping Brooklands at 79 mph with an experimental cylinder head before it was rebuilt as a sprint special with a supercharged Ulster engine equipped with an Alta aluminium cylinder head. In this form it was quick enough to win the 1100-cc class in various events and tie with E.R. Hall's formidable M.G. Midget at Shelsley Walsh in 1932. It continued to be successful wherever it was raced, even at Brooklands, with gradual improvements made until it was so good it became part of the Austin works team in 1935. By the spring of 1936 it had a special single-seater body and could run only one second off the pace of new works twin overhead camshaft Austin racers and just pip Bert Hadley's works side valve racer at Lewes!

A.N.L. MacLachlan takes his Gordon England Brooklands-based special up Shelsley Walsh after it had been re-bodied in single seater form before the war.

In other spheres, a strange Seven with a chopped-about Chummy body that had been used by the Barnes brothers before they got their works car, was purchased by a young man called Charles Metchim. The Barnes team had brutally reshaped the body to contain a nine-gallon fuel tank in the scuttle with another four-gallon tank behind the seats, for long-distance racing. All sorts of bits and pieces were cut off the body, which had been mounted on a single-seater chassis, in turn fitted with a prototype Ulster engine.

A considerable amount of development—aimed chiefly at making the car reliable—followed, with spasmodic competition between 1929 and 1932 before Metchim enjoyed a successful season in domestic events (including the Land's End Trial). But with this meagre experience, he still managed to get an entry in the 1933 Le Mans 24-hour race!

A single large Solex carburettor was retained on the unsupercharged engine, with a gallon aluminium sump and an extra large water radiator. Problems with getting a support team together resulted in Austin development engineer John Appleton becoming co-driver with a Lloyds broker, Ted Lindon, as mechanic. Calculations showed that the car stood a good chance of a high placing in the important Index of Performance if it could average at least 40 mph and remain within 40 per cent of the time set by two supercharged M.G. Midgets in the 750-cc class. Clutch trouble—for the first time in the car's hard life—caused a lot of consternation, before an accident in which a crashed Alfa Romeo brought down a tree near Arnage led to the Seven's downfall. Metchim was unable to stop in case he could not restart (without a clutch that would disengage), and had to plough through the tree's branches. The impact broke the nearside steering arm and although he continued for a while he was disqualified after 16 hours for having a car in a dangerous condition. But it just showed how far an impecunious amateur could go ... Metchim returned to Le Mans in 1934 when the car had been completely rebuilt in much smarter form, but had to retire with electrical trouble.

Meanwhile Sir Herbert Austin was still smarting over the way M.Gs had trounced his works Sevens in competition and taken away so many of their hard-earned records. It was during 1932 that the activities of a young man called Murray Jamieson came to light. He had been spotted performing well in an Ulster while working for tuning ace Amherst Villiers—and was promptly hired to produce an M.G.-beater when it was revealed that he had designed a new supercharger. Although the hiring of Jamieson had Sir Herbert's full approval, it was essentially Waite's project. In the meantime, the existing single-seaters were entered in races for Pat Driscoll, Goodacre and Barnes. They managed to take the team prize in the International Trophy race at Brooklands behind the winning Alfa Romeo and three of M.G.'s new 1,086-cc six-cylinder Magnettes. In the Relay race, however, they were handicapped down to fourth place although they made fastest time at 91.60 mph.

The ding-dong battle with M.G. over records continued in 1933 as Driscoll re-took the 50-kilometres at 100.24 mph, followed by 101.52 mph in one of the single-seaters before moving the 50-mile and 100-kilometre records up to 102.33 mph and 102.26 mph. But within the month, M.Gs had gone 4 mph faster ...

The first results of Jamieson's work were then seen as he brought out a new single-seater fitted with his supercharger and a distinctive new body based on Campbell's world land speed record car. In fact, it was the first Austin Seven to look like a modern racing car. The radiator was covered by a squared-off air tunnel with wide side fairings to deflect the wind around the exposed front wheels. Other fairings were formed like pontoons between the front and rear wheels and at the back. The driving position was kept as low as possible by taking the propeller shaft diagonally across the chassis to the nearside of the rear axle. The driver then sat between the propeller shaft and the offside chassis member. The steering had to be altered to clear the engine as a result, with a swinging link in the fore and aft rod. The aluminium body was kept as smooth as possible with a concealed fuel filler and vertical tunnel to feed air to the single SU carburettor. Weight saving was not taken to extremes as it was found that it affected stability adversely. In marked contrast to many other record cars, a starter motor and dynamo were retained and the instrument panel had at least 10 dials!

The engine was also fairly normal although it produced 70 bhp. It had a stiff counter-balanced crankshaft with standard steel connecting rods and a dry-

Murray Jamieson's first single seater Austin Seven featured world land speed record-style body work with pontoons between the wheels.

sump lubrication system. This featured a pump which drew oil from a dashboard tank and passed it through a cooler to the front of the crankshaft, which was hollow, with channels cut in the webs to allow the oil to reach the big ends. The camshaft took a further oil supply with a separate pipe for each lobe. A scavenging pump sucked the oil out of the crankcase and back through another cooler to the reservoir. The water radiator's header tank was mounted alongside on the scuttle to keep the nose line as low as possible. Large ducts, set low towards the rear of each pontoon, allowed the air taken in through the radiator to escape.

The cylinder head was very special, however, being made from alloy with at least 20 securing studs and a cut-out to take a water pump. Jamieson's two-bladed Roots-style supercharger was mounted upright in front of the engine with a direct drive from the crankshaft. A propeller-driven twin-cylinder air pump beneath the radiator cowling kept up pressure in the rear-mounted fuel tank with a safety valve on the instrument panel, supplemented by a hand-pump. Ignition was by an asbestos-shielded magneto to twin sparking plugs from a distributor mounted over the flywheel. The rest of the car was more or less standard, although the clutch pedal was rearranged to give it more leverage.

Jamieson had high hopes of seeing 120 mph from this car, but was agonisingly short of his target at 119.38 mph for the five miles, 119.39 mph for 10 km and 119.19 mph for 10 miles at Montlhery. These times were enough to beat Eyston's M.G. records, until Eyston had the frontal area of his Magic Midget reduced. It then became too small for him to squeeze into, and his co-driver, Bert Denly, had to take over to put the records up to between 125 and 128 mph. Even a Jamieson reply, in which he improved an M.G. record of 105.76 mph for the 50 km to 113.47 mph was promptly countered.

But further work on the Austin's supercharger gave it an extra 5 bhp, and with a longer tail for better streamlining, Jamieson at last extracted 120 mph. It

It was subsequently developed with a longer tail and disc wheel covers to become the first side valve car to exceed 120mph on a two-way run. Murray Jamieson is pictured in the car which would be driven by Pat Driscoll.

became the first side-valve car to exceed that speed on a two-way run, with Driscoll at the wheel recording 122.74 mph for the flying kilometre on Southport beach in March 1934.

Its object achieved, the side-valve record car was then used as the basis of a new circuit racer. The engine, blower and three-speed offset transmission, special steering gear and dry-sump lubrication system, were transferred to a new chassis with as much weight saved as possible. An ultra-lightweight bodyshell was built without the bulky side pontoons and to lines that would be similar to those of the brand-new cars on which Jamieson was working. This car, which weighed only 8.5 cwt, also featured a new tubular front axle which had a transverse leaf spring beneath it.

Driscoll took third place in a Brooklands handicap first time out, beating 'Hammy' Hamilton's Mountain circuit lap record in an M.G. by just 0.4 seconds. But he was then beaten by another M.G., driven by D.N. Letts, by 0.2 seconds at Shelsley Walsh!

In later races at Brooklands, Driscoll broke the Mountain record repeatedly, to leave it at 73.64 mph before a new Q-type M.G. managed 74.58 mph. Then the same thing happened to the standing-start kilometre and mile records set by the German driver Eugen Burggaller at 73.4 and 83.5 mph in a similar car to that of Driscoll. A private team of ex-works single-seaters, run by W.L. Thompson, was successful in circuit racing, their most notable victory being in the Relay race.

Encouraged by this reasonable showing for a season against the very highly-developed M.G.s, Austin then built another side-valve single-seater with a more streamlined nose cowling for 1935, as work progressed on their brand-new cars.

But no sooner had the new side-valve car been completed and won its class for Driscoll at Shelsley Walsh than work on a new front axle was completed. The tubular beam was sawn in half and reconnected by a roller bearing to give some

George Duller partnered Charlie Goodacre to race this super charged single seater Austin Seven in the 1933 Brooklands 500-mile race, but they had to retire with a mystery misfire.

measure of independent suspension to each front wheel. Driscoll found that this modification alone was worth an extra 15 mph on the tricky banked turn of the Mountain circuit...

But these side-valve cars still struggled against the faster-developing M.Gs and success was scant in 1935 although Driscoll managed to regain the standing-start kilometre and mile records for a few weeks at 77.43 and 85.97 mph. The season served to bring two new drivers to the team; Charlie Dodson and Stanley Woods, who were alike in that they had both performed exceptionally well on motor cycles.

Although a new road circuit had been opened at Donington, its parkland roads were still rather narrow for racing and only the occasional foray was allowed at the slow and twisty Crystal Palace circuit. Hill climbing simply meant Shelsley Walsh, until Prescott was opened in 1938.

As a result, club racing of the type that goes on almost every weekend in Britain today was almost non-existent, because there was no ready supply of redundant airfields to provide cheap and easy circuits. This meant that trials held off the road on a variety of tracks, which were in plentiful supply in Britain in the 1930s, assumed great importance. The classic events, such as the Land's End, were too ambitious to organise every weekend, so one-day 'sporting' trials became highly popular. A typical event attracted an entry of up to 150, 'observed' hills, or non-stop sections being laid out with fiendish delight. The predominant element on grass-covered cart tracks, disused bridle paths and old 'Roman' roads was MUD! Such tortuous tests were scattered over a fairly wide area, so the cars had to be fully road-equipped to travel between them. This meant that they varied from standard sports cars to lightly-modified examples.

Visibility was of prime importance in such events, so a wide variety of open Austin Sevens were used, although there was the occasional saloon; their rivals were, as ever, M.Gs, plus Singer sports cars, 'chain gang' Frazer Nashes, Rileys and Triumphs and eventually such exotics as Frazer Nash-BMWs, stark Allard specials and the new four-wheeler Morgans. Until 1938, the main aid to progress through seemingly never-ending mud were knobbly tyres, with almost every car carrying at least two spare wheels so equipped, with centre-locking to make changing easier.

These conditions bred intense inter-marque rivalry with fiercely devoted fans of each model. Success in such events had a direct influence on sales, so factory teams were in evidence, notably the Cracker and Musketeer M.G.s, the Red, White and Blue, and Candidi Provocatores Singers, the Tailwagger Allards and the Grasshopper Austin Sevens. Officially, they belonged to the drivers, as works teams were banned to give amateurs a better chance!

Three Grasshoppers were built in 1935 in time for the Land's End Trial in

One of the first Grasshoppers built to compete in the 1935 Land's End trial.

which J. Orford gained a gold medal and W. Milton won a second-class award with R.J. Richardson making up the team of cars registered AOX3, AOX4, and AOV343. They were essentially re-bodied Speedies. The coachwork was similar to that used by Singer with a six-gallon slab tank at the back carrying a mounting for two spare wheels. Normally 3.50 × 19-inch tyres were used with deeply-notched treads for trials. The Grasshoppers had much deeper wings than normal to avoid clogging by mud and a unique radiator cowling like that on an Austin 10 sports. Fold-flat windscreens were fitted to allow the drivers maximum visibility, along with an ultra-lightweight hood that could be stowed in an instant. A matching rev counter and speedometer were fitted either side of the steering wheel with oil and water gauges, an ammeter and a clock. Further special equipment included a remote-control gearchange and a 5.5:1 rear axle ratio for most events. A Speedy-style dropped front axle was used on a van-specification heavy-duty frame.

Singer and Riley had fared well at Le Mans in 1934, with an M.G. Magnette finishing fourth, so M.G. were encouraged to enter their best-seller, the Midget, in 1935. They went for the maximum publicity with an all-woman team managed by Eyston, which meant that Austin had to enter, too—with Grasshoppers as their nearest-to-standard competition cars!

Three more Grasshoppers were built with a special Speedy along the same lines. These cars, registered BOA57, 58, 59 and 60, had lighter cycle-type wings

Bill Sewell and Rowley Appleby hard at work in the 1937 Colmore Trophy trial with their ex-Le Mans Grasshopper.

and Jamieson alloy heads like those used on the side valve racers. In the event, a big British Lagonda won, with a Riley fourth, and the M.Gs back in 24th, 25th and 26th places, followed by one of the Grasshoppers driven by Dodson and Richardson, and the Speedy in last place, driven by Carr and Barbour. These BOA-registered cars were then converted to trials specification with engines progressively modified to give more power and torque.

These engines normally used a three-bearing crankshaft with the 1.3125-inch big end bearings, and webs strengthened along Ulster lines. Two oil feeds were used, one to the centre main bearing as normal, and the other by an external pipe from the main gallery to a nose piece in the manner of a pressure-fed two-bearing engine. The pressure on this system was more than 30 psi.

A Nippy one-gallon ribbed alloy sump was used with thinwall bearings, deep, fully-machined, H-section connecting rods and very light slipper pistons.

The water passages in the cylinder block were enlarged with special porting to the Nippy-style inlet and exhaust manifolds.

Each cylinder had two external ribs on its bore sides with the block being secured to the crankcase by 0.375-inch studs. Their alloy cylinder heads with long central cast water outlets were retained by similar studs. Sparking plugs of 14 mm diameter were placed over the exhaust valves, which were slightly smaller than the inlets.

The valves were longer than those on an Ulster with double springs and short tappets. The camshaft was of a very high-lift pattern with a steel driving gear which meshed with another in a special dynamo housing. The dynamo drive was fitted with a pulley which powered, by belt, a Type 125 Centric supercharger of the sort that was becoming popular on competition M.Gs. This ran at a maximum of 6 psi in conjunction with a large vertical Stromberg carburettor. In this adaptation, Austin found that a very thin 0.03125-inch copper and asbestos cylinder head gasket worked well.

Four more Grasshoppers, registered COA118, 119, 120 and 121 were built for Le Mans in 1936 and three of them entered again in 1937 after industrial unrest had led to the cancellation of the 1936 event. These cars were substantially the same as the earlier ones, the chief difference being in the use of 17-inch wheels to give better handling. Unfortunately, all three cars, driven by Goodacre/Buckley, Petre/Mangen and Dodson/Hadley, were eliminated with lubrication problems, but they ran well enough to take reasonably high placings in the Donington 12 hours which followed. They were then converted to trials specification.

By the time the new Austin Seven racer appeared in March 1936 it was something of an anti-climax because M.G. had been forced to give up racing, the cost in time and development having become too high. The new Austin cost a fortune too because it was so advanced!

Essentially, Jamieson had designed a highly-supercharged twin overhead cam hemi-head engine of only 744 cc capacity that was stressed to run up to 14500 rpm to produce more than 120 bhp! He visualised a beautiful little car for this engine with independent suspension all round (rather like a project on which M.G. were working before it was axed), but there was considerable pressure over the time it took to develop, so he had to compromise with the existing front suspension from the side-valve racer and a solid rear axle carried by quarter elliptic springs and radius rods. The chassis was also a simple twin channel affair, but the engine was a work of art.

The light alloy cylinder head and camshaft housings were cast in one piece and the cylinder block and crankcase in another. All other unstressed parts were made from elektron to keep down their weight. At first glance, the camshafts dominated the engine because they were huge, fully 2 inches wide, each running in three bearings. Their sheer size was dictated by the necessity of using triple springs with a combined tension of 550 psi to operate each valve. The valves were inclined at 90 degrees to each other with a 14-mm sparking plug in the centre of the combustion chamber. The camshafts, and everything else, were

Jamieson loved to drive his cars, undertaking much of the test work in the twin-cam machine.

driven from the back of the engine by a train of 11 gears for maximum precision. Jamieson's famous blower was built into this train to run at 1.5 times engine speed, raising the boost to 20 psi through an enormous SU carburettor.

Nitrided wet liners were used for the cylinders which projected into the head with detachable water jackets. The crankshaft was machined from the solid with a plain bearing in the centre and roller bearings at either end. The connecting rods and pistons followed established Austin racing practice with a bore and stroke of 60.32 mm × 65.09 mm (which, translated into the old English measures to which Austin worked at the time, was $2\frac{3}{8}$ ins × $2\frac{9}{16}$ ins). Part of the gear train from the crankshaft drove a water pump and a Scintilla magneto, with a side-mounted starting handle operating through them. Full dry-sump lubrication was used with a triple pump having high and low pressure sections as well as scavenging, being fed from two three-gallon tanks mounted on either side of the propeller shaft. A beautifully-made oil cooler with tubes only 0.0006 ins in diameter ensured the maximum surface exposure to the airstream in its position up front with the water radiator. This engine was built initially with white metal bearings—which were quite conventional at the time—which restricted revs to 8500 and the power output to 116 bhp. But this was good enough for 121 mph flat out in 6000 miles of testing at Donington and there was a built-in capacity for the larger crankshaft and connecting rods which would have been needed for higher revs.

The offset transmission, which absorbed a fair amount of power, was replaced with an in-line design that used double reduction gears from an engine mounted as low as possible to keep down the frontal area and the centre of gravity. This was especially important because it was a relatively tall unit with its twin overhead cams, carrying a large proportion of its weight at the top; hence the side-mounted starting handle. There was not enough room to swing a handle had it been mounted in the conventional position in line with the front of the crankshaft. A single-plate racing clutch at the other end had no less than five toggles and fifteen springs to convey the engine's power to a four-speed gearbox built-in unit. Synchromesh was used on the top three gears with a remote change under the driver's left hand. The propeller shaft had two universal joints to bring it into a supporting bearing in a crosspiece under the driver's seat, with a torque tube running from there to the rear axle. This had another supporting bearing to stop it from whipping at high revs. The body was substantially similar to that of the side-valve racers with a higher tail to cover a larger 25-gallon fuel tank as the fuel consumption had risen to 7.5mpg for long-distance races despite a 7,600-rpm limit, with between 3.5 and 4 mpg in sprints when 9,400 rpm could be used. The steering box was set in the scuttle with a fore and aft shaft to a bell crank, which connected to a link for the steering arm. Cable-operated brakes were used with 12-inch drums at the front and 10-inch ones at the rear, along with 5.25 inch X 16 inch alloy-rimmed racing wheels.

Three of these very advanced cars were built and it is not surprising that they suffered from various teething troubles in their first year. Fortunately the side-valve cars had become reasonably reliable by then and provided a good back-up team. In fact, the German driver Walter Baumer managed to beat all the twin cam cars with a side-valve racer at Shelsley Walsh in June, which did not amuse the newly-created Baron Austin! Next month, however, two of the twin cam cars, driven by Dodson and Driscoll, made up the winning team with

Walter Baumer prepares for a historic ascent of Shelsley Walsh in June 1936 in which he recorded 42.6 seconds with his side-valve Seven to beat all the works twin cam cars.

Bert Hadley in a side valve at the Macclesfield speed trials. But a few days later Driscoll was badly hurt in a crash at the Blackwell Hill House climb which resulted in one of the twin cam cars being written off. The accident happened in treacherously wet conditions when the steering broke, and years later Driscoll said that the twin cam machines handled magnificently and cornered as well in the wet as the dry.

Record-breaking was far more rewarding for the new cars in 1936. Dodson set new records for the Brooklands outer and Mountain circuits that would stand for ever at 121.14 and 77.02 mph before taking a whole string of 750-cc records from 1 km to 100 miles at speeds up to 121.21 mph. By then, however, Austin was again considering quitting motor racing, so engine development came to a halt without the cars reaching their objective: M.G's flying mile record of 130.51 mph.

But so much money had been spent on twin cam development that it seemed wasteful not to run the cars again in 1937 with only minor modifications. This season turned out to be a good deal more successful with Hadley winning at Donington, Crystal Palace and the 1100-cc class in the Brighton Speed Trials. In addition, Goodacre won the Coronation Trophy race at Donington

By 1937 the twin cam races were proven to be more successful with Bert Hadley running as the hare in the Coronation Trophy race at Donington. He was eliminated by a fractured oil pipe, but the race was won by his team mate Charlie Goodacre.

and Kay Petre took the ladies' record at Shelsley Walsh with a side valve car.

Meanwhile the Relay race had been having a difficult time as even 270 miles proved too much for many of the competitors. Entries fell even when the 1500-cc limit was abandoned in 1936. This was partly because new safety standards at Brooklands tended to outlaw cars of more than 10 years old. A team of Aston Martins won in 1936 then, in 1937, in a further attempt to attract a good entry, the event was raised to international status. Austin entered the two remaining twin cam cars for Hadley and Goodacre with Mrs Petre in her side valve car. Hadley drove brilliantly, reaching more than 130 mph as he swooped down to the Railway Straight, handing over to Goodacre who moved up to fifth place in the handicap race. From there Kay Petre progressed to the lead to win by five minutes—a great victory for the team at an average speed of 105.63 mph for the 250 km.

Now problems with pistons and the fuel feed had been cured, the Austins performed well at Shelsley Walsh, Hadley breaking the 750-cc record with a 40.83-second climb, less than 2 seconds slower than Raymond Mays's outright record in a 1.5-litre ERA. Goodacre then went on to record 40.70 seconds three months later. Soon after Hadley was helping a new team of Grasshoppers, registered BOA57, 58 and 60, to numerous successes with C.D. Bradley and W.H. Scriven.

Donington and Shelsley Walsh again provided the works cars with major successes in 1938. Dodson took the British Empire Trophy race at 69.92 mph, a far higher average and over a greater distance than the winning ERA in 1937. Then Hadley lowered his Shelsley Walsh record to 40.09 seconds before taking second place in the British Empire Trophy race in 1939.

During all this activity by works cars, enthusiastic amateurs were building all manner of Austin Seven specials, chiefly for trials. One of the most ingenious was constructed by E.G. Smith around, at first, a 1928 Gordon England Cup model. Initially this had a lightened flywheel, double valve springs and a Ricardo alloy head before the chassis was substituted by another from a 1931 two-seater. An additional Ariel three-speed gearbox was then fitted behind the Austin transmission. In this form it proved rather underpowered for the most testing trials and an Ulster engine and close-ratio gearbox replaced the original, along with a home-made divided front axle to give independent suspension. Most trials hills were then taken in bottom gear on the Ariel box and top on the Ulster, although bottom/bottom had to be used occasionally! In this form the Smith Special proved capable of climbing such fearsome hills as Simms, Fingle Bridge, Doverhay, Ham, Breakheart and Cussop-Dingle, although Widlake and some of the more slippery Kentish chalk hills defeated it. The Ulster engine was invariably run at 4,000 rpm while climbing, until the crankshaft broke. The car was then converted into a three-wheeler to run in motor-cycle events, using largely single front wheel suspension from Raleigh's Austin Seven-engined van. But the original parts were retained so that it could be rapidly converted back into a car for four-wheeled events!

The majority of sporting-minded Austin Seven owners drove more standard models, however, as can be seen from the original entry list for the 750 Club's first Committee Cup trial in Kent in June 1939. It was made up of five Nippys, three Ulsters, a four-seater, a Ruby saloon, an Eight, two AEWs, an Arrow, a Brooklands two-seater, an Army two-seater, and two Chummies, plus Smith's special, and two other specials, one of which was a Williams.

A typical W-Special built by Bill Williams of Auto Conversions was based on an Ulster with a high-lift camshaft so that it would put up a reasonable performance on the occasions it was required to run without a supercharger. Williams's own machine had a special Arnott carburettor which was very much like a normal SU except that it had an advantage in that the mixture was more easily adjustable. An extra large Wolseley Hornet radiator was used that had to be partly blanked off even when the engine was running without a fan. A much-lightened flywheel was preferred with heavy-duty springs for the clutch and a close-ratio four-speed gearbox. The normal rear axle ratio was 4.9:1, although 5.25 and 5.67:1 were used sometimes. The front axle was lowered 2 ins and widened to produce a track of 3 ft 10 ins with reverse camber rear springs having extra clips to prevent spreading. The brakes were given a Bowdenex conversion and the 16-inch pressed steel wheels from a Big Seven were preferred to the lighter wire wheels because they enabled wider tyres to be used, 4.75 ins at the front and 5.25 ins at the back. These wheels fitted the normal hubs when the dowels were removed from the brake drums. Williams's special was fitted with a very narrow aluminium body carrying its spare wheel on the offside.

It was into an era of machines like this, which had survived the war, that Colin Chapman stepped with his first Lotus in 1947. The basis was a 1930 Austin Seven fabric saloon that had spent the war-time years on bricks in an old lady's front garden. This car was stripped down to the last nut and bolt and the main chassis members boxed in for extra strength. Chapman got rid of the car's inherent oversteer by turning the rear axle upside down and flattening the springs so that ground clearance was not sacrificed. This was important because the end product was intended for use in sporting trials. Chapman was still at university at the time and intensely interested in aircraft, so it was hardly surprising that the bodywork showed signs of aircraft practice. A stressed framework was built with three bulkheads made from alloy-bonded plywood. The rather angular body panels were then attached to it, with cycle-type wings held on by wood screws and Rawlplugs. This meant that the wings could be knocked off easily without damage during a trial and replaced just as easily! The back of the body was extended so that two extra passengers could be carried, or a lot of ballast during trials. Chapman was always particularly keen on the frontal appearance of his cars, so his first special had a neat copper sheet radiator cowling of similar shape to that on a Rolls-Royce!

The brakes were improved with a modified linkage and special actuating cams. Chapman could not afford much development on the engine, but it was overhauled and given a higher compression ratio and double valve springs. It was also adapted to run with a Ford downdraught carburettor by means of a special manifold.

This car was an immediate success in trials in 1948 and even more so when fitted with Ford pressed steel rear wheels so that larger tyres could be used and a split axle independent front suspension system.

By that time, Chapman had become a member of the 750 Motor Club and spent a lot of time discussing technical problems with fellow members. As a result, he decided to build his second Lotus, the Mark 2, as a dual purpose trials and circuit racing car which could still be used on the road as everyday transport.

Plate 1 The first 4,500 Austin Sevens featured a curved scuttle like this 1924 model tourer.

Plate 2 Van bodies were also mounted on the Austin Seven chassis, this 1927 model being styled to accommodate the needs of the village grocer.

Plate 3 The classic Chummy built from June 1924 had a flat-sided scuttle as fitted to this 1925 model.

Plate 4 Many Austin Sevens were equipped with special bodies, such as this 1926 Burghley sports.

Plate 5 This pretty Gordon England Cup model of 1927 is a good example of the early sporting Sevens.

Plate 6 The 1927 Super Sports was the first supercharged Austin Seven production model.

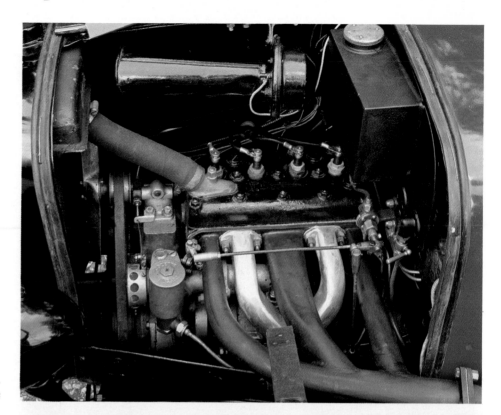

Plate 7 The belt-driven super-charger was mounted ahead of the engine in the Super Sports.

Plate 8 The engine compartment of the British Leyland Top Hat on show at Syon Park has been restored to the same immaculate condition as the rest of the car.

Plate 9 Austin's first saloon body on the Austin Seven chassis appeared in the metal in 1926. The interior was more generous than that of the tourer and soon became known as the Top Hat because of its impressive headroom and angular appearance.

Plate 10 The interior of the Top Hat saloon on display in British Leyland's museum was of excellent quality.

Plate 11 The Austin Seven chassis found numerous applications, including use as an Army scout car in the case of this 1932 model.

Plate 12 Other coachbuilders had more glamorous ideas; this is one of the first bodies by Swallow on a 1930 chassis before the firm expanded to produce Jaguar cars today.

Plate 13 The most exotic Austin Seven of all, one of the works twin cam racers, on show at Donington.

Plate 14 In 1932, the Austin Seven's body was improved with comfort in mind, although the traditional exposed radiator shell remained for the time being.

Plate 15 The transformation was complete by 1934 with the much more modern looking Ruby.

Plate 16 Delightful variations continued to be marketed on the established theme, including the cabriolet model in 1937.

Plate 17 And there was still room for a two-seater tourer right to the end of production.

Plate 18 Many specials were constructed from Austin Seven components, including this pretty example with alloy wheels.

Plate 19 Others were not so pretty, such as this 'racer' from the early 1950s, but just as charming.

Plate 20 1934 Austin Seven Speedy.

Plate 21 Some of the bodywork fitted to Austin Sevens has been quite extraordinary, like this 1924 model raced by Miss J. Arnold-Foster, pictured at Silverstone in 1982.

Plate 22 The supercharged Austin Seven of A. Nye, seen at Silverstone in 1984, really is as fast as it looks.

Plate 23 Classic trials—based on the earliest car rallies—have long been an Austin Seven preserve with some of the best displays put up by Sue Halkyard, pictured at Fingle Bridge in the 1984 London-to-Exeter.

Plate 24 The right crowd and no crowding they used to say—but plenty of hustle and bustle at the Vintage Sports-Car Club's winter driving tests on the remaining bankings of the old Brooklands motor racing circuit in 1983.

Plate 25 The VSCC's Cadwell Park meeting is also a classic—and a source of great joy for this Austineer as he swoops down one of the numerous descents.

Plate 26 The sound and the fury ... one of the reproduction side valve racers in action at Shelsley Walsh.

Plate 27 For other enthusiasts less attracted to racing, there are events like the Bristol club's spring weekend, with long open road sessions, convivial meal halts, camping and songs in the pub.

Once again, the main members of an Austin Seven's chassis was boxed in, but this time the cross members were removed and tubular braces welded in to make the structure more rigid. A split Ford 10 front axle was used and the Austin Seven rear axle retained with a 4.55:1 ratio made by forcibly meshing the 9-tooth pinion from a 4.9:1 set of gears with the 42-tooth crownwheel from a 5.125:1. Lapping-in was accomplished on a 50-mile run with the axle casing full of Bluebell metal polish! Ford pressed steel wheels were fitted all round with large-section tyres, and a Ford 8 engine was mated to an Austin Seven's four-speed gearbox by a special cast alloy adaptor plate. A body along similar lines to that of the first car was run without a radiator cowling until Chapman could afford to have one beaten from aluminium sheet. It then bore a close resemblance to that of his well-known Lotus Mark 6. But the Lotus Mark 2 was eventually fitted with an 1172-cc Ford 10 engine and provided Chapman with a highly-successful season in 1950. Many of the events were trials because of petrol shortages which had persisted since the end of the Second World War. But a number of airfields that had been built for use in the war were starting to be used for occasional motor racing—notably Silverstone in Northants, Snetterton in Norfolk, Goodwood in Sussex and Thruxton in Hampshire. Chapman qualified in a one-hour speed trial at Silverstone for the Eight Clubs' scratch race and enjoyed a 'terrific scrap' with Dudley Gahagan's Type 37 Bugatti. He also managed to win the 750 MC's Bisley Rally and a similar road event run by the North London Enthusiasts' Club to demonstrate the versatility of his Mark 2 Lotus.

Meanwhile, Holland Birkett, one of the founder members of the 750 MC, managed to get the Relay race going again at Silverstone in 1951. He framed the regulations around the last events at the now-defunct Brooklands track, which meant that competing cars had to be based closely on production machines rather than outright racers. It was appropriate: the Austin Sevens which formed the backbone of his club had done most of the winning before the war.

Yet thanks to stringent handicapping, initially by journalist Charles Bulmer, they didn't do much afterwards, despite making up the majority of the field. Such specials were also some of the most popular machines in competition at the time, so the club was able to run its Relay race at a prime time in August.

The atmosphere at Silverstone was rather more informal in those days than it is now. The pits for the Relay race consisted of a line of straw bales dividing off part of a runway near Woodcote corner. Spectators sat on the bales and the winning vintage Bentleys (which had given Davis such a hard run at Brooklands) were called in by a sign depicting a pint of beer!

Chapman was taking motor racing more seriously, though, and had decided to concentrate on circuit events rather than the more light-hearted trials. As a result he went into partnership with the brothers Michael and Nigel Allen on 1 January, 1951, to build a Lotus Mark 3 to compete in the new 750 Formula, run by the 750 MC. This formula laid down that a car had to comply with road regulations and have a cockpit at least 32 ins wide inside; the cylinder block, crankcase, gearbox casing, complete rear axle, and main chassis members had to come from a normal production Austin Seven; the engine could be overbored by only 0.060 ins and overhead cam conversions and superchargers were banned; it also had to have a starter motor, battery and dynamo and to run on pump fuel. To comply with these regulations, Chapman and the Allens took a 6 ft 9-inch wheelbase chassis and fitted it with extensions to take Newton shock absorber struts. The rear springs were flattened and given a softer rate than normal because Chapman was already years ahead of most other constructors in suspension design. He realised that better handling could be obtained by using a stiff frame and soft, well-damped, springs rather than a whippy frame and stiff springs, which had been the norm since about 1900! A 4.9:1 rear axle ratio was used because the weight of this car—intended only for circuit racing and the road—was being kept to the minimum. A late-type Ruby propeller shaft was used with a remote-control Nippy gearbox and a standard clutch which had slightly stiffer springs. The flywheel was lightened for better response and the front suspension provided by a split Ford 8 front axle which had its transverse leaf spring mounted on top. Newton struts were again used at the front, with the existing Ford 8 radius arms being retained for location. The 4-ft track axle weighed more than that of the Austin Seven, but it was preferred for having stronger kingpins. An Austin Seven steering box was mounted on its side ahead of the axle line and operated through a transverse link and separate track rods. Lockheed hydraulic brakes were fitted all round with Girling drums because they were stiffer.

At first, the chassis was fitted with a tubular scuttle hoop for additional stiffening and the Austin Seven engine was used as a stressed member, but crankcase studs started to pull out, so flexible mountings were substituted. This meant that rigidity had to be restored by a triangular brace bolted above the engine.

After early experiments with a two-bearing unit, a three-bearing engine was bored out by 0.050 ins and fitted with slightly larger inlet valves at the expense of the exhausts. A Nippy camshaft was used with Ulster springs and Covmo pistons; and then Chapman had a brainwave.

It resulted in him making a new inlet manifold that, in effect, produced a far more potent four-port cylinder head. This was achieved by grinding out the siamesed ports and and dividing them by a steel plate attached to a special inlet manifold, which carried the Stromberg twin-choke carburettor from a Ford V8. Each choke was matched to an inlet port and the exhausts were kept separate by a four-branch extractor manifold. The power output of this engine was far ahead of that of any other 750 special and the new Lotus Mark 3, with a curious bug-like alloy body, dominated the 1951 season. Such highly-tuned engines looked like being very expensive, however, so they were promptly banned by the 750 MC!

Chapman went on to produce another Austin-Ford trials special for Mike Lawson, called the Lotus Mark 4, before the rest of his early cars used mainly Ford and BMC components.

As impecunious amateurs continued to build Austin Seven specials all over the world, many were buying parts from Bill Williams, by now running Cambridge Engineering. He refused to compete against his customers in the 750 Formula, however, as he felt that his facilities and experience gave him an unfair advantage. So he built much more specialised cars for his own use in other events. One such vehicle constructed in 1957 used the Centric-blown ex-works Ulster engine from an earlier machine with a totally different frame that reflected the contemporary trends in racing sports car design. It used two main steel tubes of 2.75-inches diameter with four cross members made from the same material. A hooped scuttle section was then made up of 1-inch diameter tubing braced by 0.625-inch tubes. Independent suspension was used all round with double tubular wishbones and Newton struts. Williams also made the rack and pinion steering with his own cast alloy housing and steel gears. The rear axle consisted of an Austin Seven banjo centre section mounted rigidly in the frame connected to universally-jointed halfshafts and a torque tube locating on one of the crossmembers. A 1931 final drive was chosen because Williams could supply 4.9:1, 5.1, 5.25 and 5.66 ratios for this unit. A shortened propeller shaft allowed the engine and remote control Nippy gearbox to be mounted much further back than in a normal Austin Seven frame. Alfin brake drums were used in conjunction with a Morris Minor-based two leading shoe mechanism, and 15-inch wire wheels carrying 4.5-inch wide racing tyres. The aluminium body followed the lines of streamlined examples used on contemporary M.G. and Coventry-Climax-powered Lotuses.

Meanwhile, Jem Marsh of another Austin Seven tuning firm, Speedex, was going well in 750 Formula events, winning the Goodacre Trophy in 1959 for the most successful car. His Speedex Special was based on a boxed-in 1933 Austin Seven chassis which had been strengthened by a tubular steel crossmember and diagonal bracing. The Lotus Mark 6-style body was made from aluminium panelling welded to a framework of numerous small tubes attached to the chassis at many points, making it far more rigid. This car also featured a unique bolt-on independent front suspension system that answered all the 750 Formula competitor's prayers in one unit! It consisted of fabricated uprights and single tubular wishbones with a central mounting bracket that supported a transverse leaf spring. A rectangular bracket was bolted on top to support both tubular shock absorbers and a water pump mounting, with a track rod running round the back. Amazingly, no modifications were needed to the standard chassis! Speedex used a Nippy-based engine with pressure lubrication and their own alloy cylinder head, plus a Ford water pump. Morris Minor-inspired brakes were adopted with special Speedex alloy wheels.

Marsh then went on to build his first Marcos and use the 750 MC's Relay race as its testing round in 1960. This event had increased in importance by leaps and bounds then.

Back in 1953, the pits wall had been just a line of oil drums with 170 drivers fighting it out in everything from 750 specials to full-race Jaguar XK120s. At least one Ford Popular heralded thrills to come. It ran in what amounted to

Group Two specification with a twin carburettor 10 hp engine, cutaway wooden doors and celluloid windows to save weight.

Lest boredom should set in, 'Holly' Birkett devised a new circuit the following year. The race still started at the exit of Woodcote, and rounded Copse, but it then turned sharp right at Maggots to a hairpin at Club, before returning the same way to turn onto today's club straight and back to Woodcote. Cars travelling in opposite directions were separated by straw bales hauled in by a farmer called Baker. He then removed the windscreen from his Land-Rover, along with the air cleaner, and with a straight-through exhaust and balanced wheels, proceeded to dominate the race!

With such guaranteed spectacles, the crowds were up to latter-day grand prix standards in 1955, with top-line racing cars as a result. Lister-Bristols fought it out with Austin-Healey 100Ss, although there were still the 750 specials.

The differences in speed of such vehicles was such that only experienced drivers were accepted in 1956. Everything became more serious, even if competitors were often driving relatively mundane machines. By then the Goodwood Nine Hours had disappeared and the National Relay, as it was known, had become Britain's longest race and was the next best thing to Le Mans in 1959. All that nonsense with straw bales was out, and today's Club circuit was used. The cars were still fascinating, however ... Goggomobil GTs fought it out with D type Jaguars that were still racing at Le Mans and the perpetual 750 Formula cars.

Meanwhile trials began to follow two completely different paths, a division which had started in 1938 when persistent complaints about competitors using the same hills and lanes weekend after weekend led to the organisers adopting a deliberately low profile. The classic trials, such as the Exeter, Land's End and the Edinburgh, continued substantially unchanged, but the others became more confined sticking, where possible, to private land. Once it became no longer necessary to drive between hills on public roads, the cars became much more specialised and, as a result, the slopes even steeper and more tortuous. Competitors in this new form of 'sporting trial' had just as much fun in a far more confined space. Their cars had to become even more manoeuvrable with the result that they adopted front axles with the most incredible steering lock. By 1960, 'fiddle brakes', where one rear wheel could be stopped with an individual handbrake while the other was spun for maximum traction, had become popular. Austin Seven specials consisting of little more than an engine and transmission set as far back as possible to aid traction, dominated the 850-cc class, particularly in the hands of Rex Chappell.

During the 1960s, the 750 MC stuck to its principles of running low-cost motor sport although the once cheap and plentiful supply of Austin Seven parts was drying up. Gradually 750 racers acquired more non-Austin parts and eventually moved over to Reliant engines from 1966. These all-alloy units were built by a firm which had taken over the design of the Raleigh three-wheeler made between 1933 and 1936 which was powered by an Austin Seven engine;

and their new overhead-valve engine still owed a great deal to the original Austin design. This made it a natural transition for the 750 special builders. The club's 1172 formula also ran into similar problems once the Ford side-valve engine went out of production and it had to be replaced by formulae for first, 1200 cc, and then 1300 cc, Ford engines. Events continued to be organised for Austin Sevens and specials by the 750 MC, however, but mostly to a handicap system because the performance of surviving cars varied so much. The Austin Seven naturally found a place in Vintage Sports-Car Club events, too. But the race in which they all met was still the Relay.

The modern-day Austin Seven, the Mini, was one of the star performers in the early 1960s when a fellow called John Whitmore started a fashion for cornering them sideways. At first they threw wheels and when better ones were found it looked as though they might make the Relay their own until Colin Chapman, hovering on the edge of a financial crisis, drove a Formula Junior racing car disguised as a Lotus Seven to practically set the track alight in 1962. But Club Lotus didn't win thanks to an alert handicapper!

After that the National Relay lost much of its attraction for works participants. Holly Birkett died in 1963 and the race became his memorial as Britain's oldest and most unusual club event, the Birkett Six-Hour, in 1964. The drivers and cars were not to be trifled with, however. John Fitzpatrick drove a 'front-line' Mini and Mo Nunn chased Ferrari 250GTOs with his Porsche 904.

Something had to give and the 750 specials won their own race in 1965, due allowance having been made for their small fuel tanks. A team of factory Triumph Spitfires became one of the last works teams to contest the event. During the late 1960s, however, numerous ex-works GT cars appeared with hoards of Clubmen's machines, inspired by the example of Chapman's first production car, the Lotus Mark 6, and bearing a close resemblance to the 750 MC's new Formula 1200 cars. As prodsports became modsports, even stranger sights appeared, including the bulky frames of Gerry Marshall and Brian Muir throwing Vauxhall Vivas around with abandon ... with competition from Mike Wilds in a London Special Builders' DRW Mark 1!

A team of Aston Martins, members of whose club had been supporting the race from the very start, won again in their jubilee year, 1970, by yards from a mass of modsports M.G. Midgets, but there were hardly any spectators now. There were many more events to attract their money and the Birkett Six-Hour was hard to follow for the uninitiated. Silverstone was otherwise occupied with a Formula 5000 race in 1971 and the Relay had to move to the British Automobile Racing Club's home, Thruxton, for a year. But at least the event was in good hands: this was the club that started at Brooklands. Silverstone was a more attractive circuit for a race needing a lot of pitwork, however, and the Relay went back there the next year with an October date that meant a midday start and a 6 pm finish rather than the traditional 7 pm. It also acquired a scratch category in deference to whatever spectators it could get, and to give the fast teams something else to race for. Chevron B8s fresh from international racing fought it out with Ford GT40s from Le Mans. And so it went on until Silverstone needed resurfacing in 1977 and the late-season classic had to move to a new circuit, Donington, based in the same park used before the war; and in a museum beside the racetrack, stood the surviving Austin Seven twin cam cars...

The racing there was as good as ever, but the Relay is back at Silverstone now, on the same Club circuit, with the same incredible variety of cars, the same amazing closing speeds, and a sad lack of spectators. But there are people who will tell you that, like Brooklands of old, it's the right crowd and no crowding, watching one of the most fascinating races in the world, always with an incredible variety of Austin Sevens.

The return to Shelsley ... Terry McGrath storms up the famous hill in his reproduction side-valve Austin Seven racing car in the Vintage Sports-Car Club's Golden Jubilee meeting in 1984.

One of the neatest vintage specials in British competition ... F. Hernandez prepares to ascend Shelsley Walsh at the 1984 Golden Jubilee meeting.

One of the prettiest Austin Seven specials in Britain today ... Stuart Wood's Wragg replica single-seater, pictured at Silverstone's VSCC meeting in April 1984.

Donald Ulph's Williams Special Austin Seven—pictured at Donington and Silverstone in 1982.

E. Marriott's lovely little Austin Seven single-seater racing car—pictured at Silverstone in 1982—is based on a 1937 car.

R.J. Campbell's single-seater, pictured at Thruxton in 1983, looks for all the world like a pre-war Austin Seven, but is powered by a Fiat engine of equal vintage!

MacLachlan continued to campaign his special after the 1939-45 war, being pictured here at the VSCC's Luton Hoo hill climb in March 1948.

Trials have always been a great preserve for the Austin Seven, this saloon being put through its paces on the Exeter in 1960.

One of the most enthusiastic Austin Seven entrants in classic trials is Sue Halkyard, pictured with her Chummy at Cricket St Thomas and Fingle Bridge on the 1984 Exeter.

A fabric saloon-born competitor tackles a trial without a care in the world!

Circuit racing has, on occasions, offered unrivalled opportunities for the legendary impecunious enthusiast, seen here tackling one of the first meetings held at Brands Hatch in 1951.

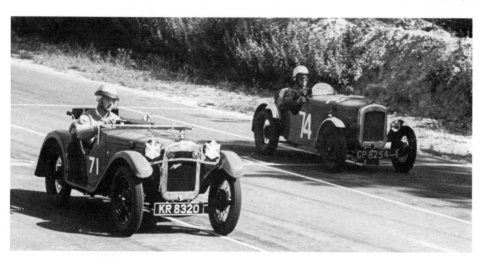

Austin Sevens are great survivors: this 1928 model was drastically modified to compete in the Nottingham Sports Car Club's race meeting at Silverstone in August 1954, vanishing for 20 or 30 years to reappear and shed its gearlever on the Bristol Austin Seven Club's 1984 spring run in the mountains of Wales.

Austin Seven racing continued with hardly a change in the 1960s, these competitors having been pictured at Cadwell Park in 1965 ... but it could have been almost any year from 1935 to 1985.

Well-known Austin Seven enthusiast B.M. Clarke is pictured in action at the VSCC Prescott meeting in August 1967.

Austin Sevens have been ever present in the Six-Hour Relay race, this
special leading a post-war replacement, an Austin A35 van, at Silverstone in 1959.

750 Formula events have always
attracted some strange specials,
none more so than M.A. Boswell's
GT, pictured at Brands Hatch in
May 1967.

Driving tests are always popular with Austin Seven enthusiasts, as demonstrated by these competitors.

Driving tests can be held almost anywhere ... even on the remains of the historic bankings at Brooklands for the VSCC members in January 1983.

Some things hardly change from one decade to the next, such as the VSCC driving tests at Enstone Airfield ... or the December weather which is frequently very murky, but not bad enough to deter such hardy entrants.

Teeth chattering in the cold, or kicking up the dust on a hot summer's day, an open Austin Seven makes ideal sport.

Sporting trials were also the preserve of Austin Sevens for years.

Some very pretty bodies were offered for Austin Seven specials after the war, including this HWM-inspired glass fibre edition on Miss Sally-Ann Brooks's car at Prescott in April 1984.

Spring special ... John Way in action with his Austin Seven at the Brighton Speed Trials in 1984.

Everybody races everybody else in some VSCC events, leading to such stirring sights as this Austin Seven cornering almost in the lee of R.A. Collings's vast 1903 Grand Prix Mercedes.

The eternal Austin Seven special ... M. Pilgrim's car was one of the fastest competing at the VSCC Donington meeting in May 1982.

There's no shortage of drama as this special leaves the pits at Silverstone in 1982.

The VSCC Cadwell Park race meeting is one of the most spectacular historic events in Britain on a circuit that has hardly changed since the 1950s—with Austin Sevens providing some of the most consistent competition. The cars pictured in 1983 were driven by A. McBeath (number 130), F. Hernandez (number 64), Simon Smith (number 117), Mrs S.M. Woodrow (number 134) and Miss J. Arnold-Forster (number 131).

Side by side by ... Silverstone, 1982, with these two Austin Sevens representing the epitome of club racing.

Mrs D.M. Threlfell shows her resolve as she takes her Austin Seven special through the chicane at Donington in 1982.

Cool, calm and collected ... and Austin Seven-born, R.P. Waller at Donington in 1982.

Austin Sevens were among the backbone of cars racing at the VSCC Silverstone meeting in 1983 ... with notable examples driven by Tim Myall (number 127) and B.M. Clarke (number 105).

Austin Sevens were much in evidence at the 50th anniversary meeting of one of their spiritual homes, Donington; Simon Smith's Ulster replica and Frank Tiedeman's Ulster being among the star performers.

Austin Seven teams in the Six-Hour Relay carry, appropriately, the number seven, followed by the letters A, B, C, D, E and so on for individual members of the team. As Tim Myall hurls his Seven special through Woodcote at Silverstone in 1983 . . .

Alan McBeath took over from Myall for a spell carrying the same team sash on the bonnet of his Austin Seven special.

Don Rawson was pictured entering the pit lane at the end of his stint in the same race.

As the cars reach their pits, the team manager rushes out to tear the sash off its Velcro mounting, in this case on Kevin Martin's Seven special in the 1982 Relay.

The sash is then transferred to the car of the next team member, in this case, McBeath, in 1982.

A fresh car is then placed in the pits to await its turn in the race.

Meanwhile, behind the pits the competing cars receive attention before returning to the fray.

In some cases the attention needed can be extensive, leading to some heroic rebuilds!

Austin Sevens can be very adaptable cars, this example shedding all manner of road-going equipment in the paddock before being raced in stripped form by P. McGuire at Silverstone in 1984.

Others, such as Derek Ulph's Seven special spend all their lives as competition vehicles.

Other Austin Seven specials, whether on parade in concours events, or just parked at a race meeting, are guaranteed to attract attention.

There are numerous special occasions when you can use your Austin Seven to good effect, such as in support of the 1983 London-to-Brighton run.

But there's no substitute for the real thing ... Frank Tiedeman's Ulster in the paddock at Donington in 1983.

Portrait of the modern 750 Formula racer ... Bob Simpson's SS Reliant at Brands Hatch in 1984.

VIII
Building an Austin Seven Special

There was a delightful period of about 20 years after the Second World War in which tuning and building Austin Seven specials became almost a national pastime in Britain and many other countries where old Sevens were still a common sight. Much of this activity in Britain was centred on constructing cars to compete under 750 Formula rules, of course, but even more so as a means of simply providing an enthusiast with a sports car of a type that would have only existed otherwise in a dream. During those years, or at least up to 1960, a complete Austin Seven could still be bought for as little as £10, whereas a ready-made sports car such as a Frogeye Sprite would have cost 50 times as much! One such enthusiast, John Haynes, who later became famous for his workshop manuals and wide variety of motoring books, started his career in publishing with a guide to building just such a special. The days are gone, of course, when

John Haynes's special is pictured during the early stages of construction. The original body of this 1931 car had been removed and the cylinder block sent away to be rebored. The crankcase was still in place and the chassis and wheels had been scraped and painted.

you could buy an Austin Seven for such a small sum and remove its derelict body with a sledgehammer, but much of his advice still holds good and offers a fascinating insight into a golden era for the eternal, impecunious, enthusiast.

After detailing how to find the necessary premises in which to complete the operation—including suggesting the corner of a commercial garage for around 50 p a week—and listing the tools that would be needed, Haynes went on to cover mechanical work.

Once the bare chassis, invariably from a saloon, had been cleaned, he recommended covering everything except the springs in a light-coloured paint to ward off corrosion and show up any cracks that might develop. One of his most important modifications was to fit telescopic shock absorbers. This was a problem at the front because it was impossible to anchor the dampers straight to the axle beam; the transverse spring got in the way. A good solution was to drill and tap the 0.75-inch bolts that held the radius arms to the axle to take a 0.375-inch stud. This was locked in with two nuts that also served to keep the shock absorber clear of the spring above. The dampers were then angled in at about 45 degrees to brackets fabricated from 0.25-inch by 2-inch steel strips. These were, in turn, welded to a triangulated top support made from 1-inch tubing rather like the independent front suspension conversion made by Speedex. The height of this tube above the leaf spring and the length of its supports were governed partly by the intended lines of the body and partly by the necessity to compress the shock absorbers by about one quarter of their length. This meant that they would be half-compressed when the car was completed, said Haynes. The damper frame supports were then welded to a bottom plate which was bolted to the chassis nose piece through the holes vacated by the old friction shock absorbers.

Next Haynes recommended that any chassis extension at the back should be boxed-in with angle iron to support a 1-inch transverse steel tube above the rear axle, with more steel plating bracing the chassis legs at the back. The rear shock absorbers were then bolted to brackets welded to the brake back plates, and angled in to mountings on the transverse tube. Again, the geometry was worked out so that they were one quarter compressed on the bare chassis. The steering gear was then modified to give the column a more sporting line by bolting a Cambridge Engineering wedge between the chassis and the steering box. Haynes also recommended a Bowden cable conversion for the brakes and a 'benched' handbrake lever. This was achieved by heating up the lever, bending it at 90 degrees in the middle, and then cranking it back upright after a few inches, thus shortening the lever to work under the lower bodyline. Engine work came next:

'It is advisable to first clean the exterior of the engine, the next step being to dismantle it to ascertain what requires renewing. Remove the cylinder head and insert a feeler gauge between the piston and cylinder wall. Anything in excess of 0.003 ins ovality is wrong and the cylinders should be rebored and oversize pistons and rings fitted. Far the cheapest way to do this is to remove the block from the crankcase and to send it to a specialised firm who will send you a rebored unit in exchange. To do this remove all nuts round the base of the block, also the dynamo, and casing with fan bracket and fan in order to gain access to the front nut. Remove all valves, cotters, springs, etc, but leave the valve guides in. When the block and new pistons return, piston cuffs should be fitted in order to compress the rings and thus ensure easy replacement in the cylinder. Remember to make sure that the oil baffles which surround the connecting rods are properly aligned and seated in the crankcase. Pistons two and three should be fitted first and then numbers one and four. Remember to buy a set of new gaskets and a solid copper one for the cylinder head. After assessing the amount of wear in the bores, move on to the big ends. Remove the sump and gauze oil filter, taking care not to break the oil gasket. If there are signs of wear, and this can be detected by noting if it is possible to move the rods up and down in a vertical plane on the crankshaft, rub down the white metal-lined bearing caps on a sheet of medium grade emery cloth laid on a perfectly flat surface such as plate glass. If, however, the crankpins are excessively oval, taking them up in this manner will result in the bearings becoming very tight during part of the rotation of the crankshaft. The only answer is to have the crankpins reground, and the bearings remetalled and bored undersize. Make sure the two, or three, depending on engine year, main bearings are sound and then inspect the timing gears for wear. It is advisable to have new valves and valve guides, which can be removed with a drift and hammer or by using a nut and bolt on an extractor bracket. Refit the engine, taking great care that there is no dust or dirt between matching surfaces and that proper washers, etc, are used. The valves can then be ground in and care must be taken to ensure that no paste is left in the parts, cleaning them and the block surface with petrol and waste rag.

'To deal with modifications, the following should be completed while the engine is dismantled. If the flywheel is lightened, engine acceleration will be faster, and higher revolutions possible. In connection with higher revolutions, double valve springs are essential, to prevent valve bounce. When seating the carburettor, it must be remembered that idling speed should be kept fairly high, otherwise very rough running will be experienced. Grinding down the cylinder head to give a compression ratio of 6.8:1 will give more power and acceleration, but this modification is useless unless the engine has been rebored. A light alloy head carries the additional advantage of giving exceptionally good heat distribution, and it is possible to machine it down to give a compression ratio of 8:1. Little can be done to the lubrication system unless exceptional engineering facilities are available, but the water cooling can be modified. If a sleek graceful bodyline is visualised, it is essential to lower the radiator and this may be realised by steel brackets. These are fabricated so that they carry the radiator forward in front of the chassis nose and then down, anchorage of the bracket being on the chassis nose. As this will probably result in the failure of the thermo-siphon cooling system, it may be necessary to install a pump, electrical or mechanical, to circulate the water. I personally feel an electrical pump is easier to install, though it places an additional load on the dynamo.

'Further modifications to improve engine power and speed can be carried out through carburation and manifolding changes. First, carburation: both the Lotus-Austin and the Stoneham special (both successful competition cars) used a Stromberg carburettor and I have yet to hear of one which will surpass it for efficiency. Part of this results in exceptional acceleration, due to a pump which squirts in a jet of fuel to the engine when the throttle pedal is suddenly depressed. Running to a jet size 038, the Stoneham special was capable of 0–50 mph in 8.5 seconds, and possessed a maximum speed with an 8:1 compression ratio, light alloy head, and Ulster engine, of around 90 mph, or an engine speed of 6,000 rpm. A manifold for a Ford V8 22 hp carburettor of this type can be simply constructed from suitably curved copper tubing. There are many other carburettors and manifolds which give very good results, such as a vee-shaped manifold which will take a side-draught Austin 10 Zenith and Morris Minor SU; another vee-shaped manifold which takes a Morris 8 SU; a manifold with a built-in balance pipe for twin Morris 8 SUs and Cambridge Engineering market a four-branch tubular exhaust manifold with, if required, twin induction pipes, fitted with a matched pair of coupled and linked semi-downdraught carburettors...'

Such were the joys of the late 1950s, with exchange cylinder blocks and a wide variety of tuning gear for the Austin Seven. Haynes then went on to explain how to improve gasflow by time-honoured methods with files, emery cloth, wirewool and metal polish. He also told in detail how to make yourself a remote-control gearchange, which amounted to a duplicate gearlever mounted on the

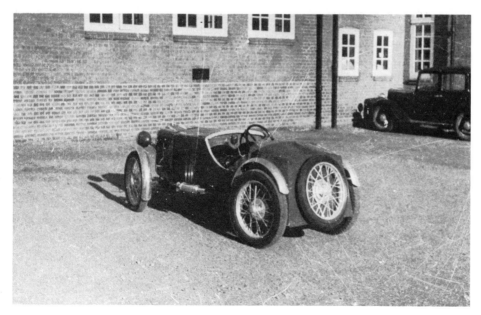

The car is shown in the quadrangle at John Haynes's school, Sutton Valence, in Kent, nearing completion and awaiting Perspex wind deflectors.

floor and connected to the existing gearlever stub by an alloy tube—far cheaper than proprietory ones. Haynes also had strong views on a special's body:

'While building a special, many people intimate that the most important item is the engine, and that a large amount of time and trouble should be spent on it. Although the engine is vitally important ... I maintain that the most important items are the chassis and body, and that the engine can have time and trouble lavished on it when the former two items are quite completed. It is the body that largely gives a "750" its individual character and also reflects its owners' technical skill and knowledge. A hotted-up engine, unless the owner has shown real initiative, merely consists of a whole lot of modifications produced by several firms, and all the owner has had to do is to attach them to his power unit.

'The body, on the other hand, unless it has been produced by a firm, is the builder's own creation, and as such he should take more care, pride and pleasure in its construction than in any other component. The engine can be removed, dismantled, and rebuilt at will, the body cannot. This is all leading up to the point, that to my mind at least, the body—during the process of constructing a special—is far the most important part. It will also largely determine the car's market value.'

Haynes said the ideal 750 special body should be strong, beautiful and useful. In his opinion, few available bodies combined all three virtues, and they were chiefly glass fibre ones. He did not recommend doors because the body sacrificed a lot of strength and rigidity if they were incorporated. At that time, of course, nobody thought of a sports car as being anything other than open! Haynes was in favour of cycle-type wings for aesthetic appeal, but warned

The young John Haynes is seen sitting happily behind the wheel of his completed car in July 1955.

against attaching them to the brake back plates. This not only increased unsprung weight, he said, but exposed the wings to a terrible battering.

He advised that panel beating should be kept to a minimum because it was a skilled operation, although pre-shaped glass fibre panels often worked well with partly aluminium-clad bodies. The idea then was to use readymade glass fibre parts, such as a nose cone, with metal sheeting where curves were not needed. Wooden body frames usually weighed little more than those using tubular steel supports. Haynes preferred steel for its strength, but pointed out that it was more difficult to fashion. The ideal aluminium sheeting would be 18 swg, although 20 swg alloy was acceptable. Unsupported edges should be turned over a length of wire to prevent them splitting, and wherever a nut and bolt was used to attach the body to its frame, a spring washer should be incorporated. 'This is, perhaps, obvious, but how often have I seen a special full of holes where nuts and bolts should be, and many of them, where fitted, without washers?' said Haynes. His ideal exhaust was chromium-plated with a motor-cycle silencer.

He said that one of the easiest bodies to construct was with an ash frame laid out around the standard saloon's bucket seats, the original steel floor, radiator and cowling. The spare wheel was carried vertically on the back with cycle-type wings supported by struts from the body sides. The number of curves in the body panels depended on the bodybuilder's skill.

Electrical conduit tubing was recommended for metal-framed bodies, with a warning against the variety which had seams: they collapsed when you tried to bend them! The easiest way of bending was to clamp the tubing in a vice and heat up the inside of the proposed curve with a welding torch. Items such as a propeller shaft tunnel could be bent over a drainpipe.

Further work was in progress on the car in December 1955 when this picture was taken at the Haynes family home in Tankerton, Kent, with, from the left: a school friend, Michael Palmer; Haynes's father, Harold; his younger brother, David; the young constructor, and his sister, Mary.

It was with books of instructions like this and proprietory glass fibre panels from a variety of sources that two generations of enthusiasts went happily on their way creating all manner of weird and wonderful devices based on the Austin Seven, and a lot of very attractive ones.

Colin Chapman's ultimate Austin Seven special, the Lotus Mark 3.

Basically standard cars were often made rather special by the substitution of smaller wheels, and perhaps, larger headlamps!

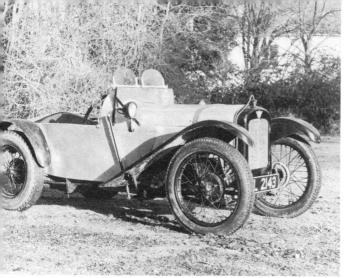
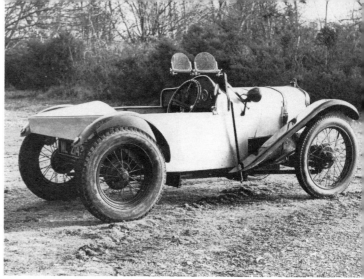

All manner of adventurous body styles were favoured on Austin Seven specials in the mid-1950s, this example being a typically workmanlike one.

Another view of the cheeky 1928 special that lost its gearlever in Wales!

A high degree of enthusiasm is needed by any Austin Seven special owner!

IX
Strengths and Weaknesses

The very fact that so many Austin Sevens survive today after sixty years' abuse shows that they have a lot of strong points. One of the most obvious, the way in which the chassis frequently remains in good condition as the rest of the car decays, is due to a weakness: the engine often sprays out so much oil that it coats the main rails with gunge that will resist almost any form of corrosion! But brakes and lights apart (which were fine for the 1920s but nothing near like good enough for the 1980s), the main thing that kills off an Austin Seven is the rusting and deterioration of the body. Other major maladies, such as a broken crankshaft, are only likely to keep the car off the road until either the owner or a subsequent purchaser can afford to repair it. But bodywork can be very expensive to repair and often leads to a car being dismantled and sold for parts. It has been proven frequently that a visit to an autojumble can locate enough parts to build a rolling chassis, giving rise to a situation where there are numerous Austin Seven chassis 'just waiting for the bodywork'.

Obviously they fall into three categories: the pre-1931 short chassis models, the 1931–34 examples with a longer wheelbase, and the pre-1934 Ruby-style cars. At present there are a variety of reproduction bodies available for the early cars, but few for those made after 1931. The reason for this contrast in readymade supplies is that the later bodies need a lot more skilled work to construct—particularly in panel-beating—and as a result they are likely to cost too much to be made on a speculative basis. Although an Austin Seven was a cheap car when it was new, it can now cost nearly as much to make a new body for it, as it does for a far more exotic, and valuable, pre-war car. The cause of this rapid escalation in Austin Seven body prices has been rises in labour rates. The cost was low before the war because Austin Seven bodies were made in large quantities, labour was cheap and they didn't need much raw material. Now they have to be handmade by skilled workers, the saving in material makes little difference to the total cost.

This is never more evident than when an Austin Seven saloon's interior needs restoration. The cost of a complete new interior, especially if much leather is needed, can be more than the cost of buying and restoring the rest of the car! Therefore, cars with good, original, interiors are especially valuable, as, indeed, are cars with good bodies. It is much easier to repair or renovate the mechanical side. Likewise, the cost of restoring a fairly decayed original body is likely to be much lower than building a completely new one.

Once a car achieves classic status, an open or sports version usually fetches more than a closed one because prospective purchasers only visualise using them on high days and holidays. The best investment is then likely to be a pre-1931 open Seven, especially because it also qualifies, in Britain, as a vintage car. Happily, this is one of the cheapest to restore or recreate! Austin Seven enthusiast, Michael Brisby, editor of *The Automobile*, a monthly magazine which caters exclusively for pre-war motoring enthusiasts, has concluded that the Gordon England Cup model is the most practical proposition in this context although there is a good trade in Ulster reproductions. The reason for this is that it is relatively easy to make an accurate copy of a Gordon England Cup model from early parts and it has an attractive appearance, whereas genuine Ulster parts are rare even if an ordinary Austin Seven can be made to look like a real Ulster by fitting a new body. The vans were outstandingly pretty, too, and make attractive reproductions, not the least because they can be a star attraction at vintage commercial events! Happily, it is also possible to buy a readymade van

One of the prettiest and most desirable Austin Sevens ... the Gordon England Cup model driven by its creator with his wife by his side.

The ultimate Austin Seven for reproduction: an Ulster replica.

body for the neglected post-1934 chassis, along with replica Arrow Foursome tourer coachwork.

Although just about everything imaginable may have decayed in a car over as many as sixty years, the fact that relatively little wood was used in the Chummy often makes it a more viable restoration project than many other models, particularly the fabric-bodied and coachbuilt saloons. It is not too difficult to restore a fabric car providing enough of the original wooden frame is left, but all too often this is not the case. Coachbuilt cars present far greater problems because they used a wooden frame too, and aluminium panels which are expensive to repair or fabricate. On the other hand, the coachbuilt cars, such as the Swallows, are highly desirable, especially for their rarity value.

There's no reason a fabric saloon
should not be reconstructed.

Apart from crumbling wooden frames and pinhole corrosion in aluminium panels, they suffer from the same basic ailments as the steel bodies: they rot all round the bottom.

When restoration is contemplated, it is wise not to fall into the temptation of removing the body from the chassis or doing the mechanical work first. Providing it has been established that the chassis is reasonably straight and the car can be made to stand squarely, it is better to remove individual panels only in one area at a time and then to gradually strengthen or replace rotten wooden frame members. As the bottom ones are more likely to be badly affected than the top, this often entails supporting the body from the top while the bottom runners—the wooden equivalents of a modern car's box-section sills—are replaced. Again, this problem is best attacked with as little dismantling as possible: if one side is completed at a time, the opposite side can often provide invaluable data during replacement. In addition, it is imperative that no parts should be destroyed, no matter how far corroded, as they may well be an aid in the remaking of a new part or show how another part was located.

In this context, a modern autofocus 35 mm camera can be invaluable. Their computerised flash systems work so well that the pictures they produce can provide an invaluable record of how a part, or an area, should look upon reassembly.

Apart from the body rockers, the other main members that are vital to a body are likely to be the scuttle area and the doorposts. They should be replaced or repaired in the same manner as the rockers. It is often found that this is a far easier task than might be expected because proper joints were rarely used in coachbuilt body frames. This is because they took longer to make: the individual members were usually simply screwed together, although there tended to be lots of slots for minor spars. In addition, glue was rarely used to hold members together because it can make a frame too rigid, causing the ash spars to split as the chassis flexes. Screws allow the little extra movement that is vital. But they also rust and can be a constant cause of trouble. When new parts are being fitted together, galvanised screws are to be recommended, along with bright-plated and brass ones. The original type of well-seasoned ash can be difficult to find today, if not impossible. Fortunately, kiln-dried ash can usually be submitted without problems if parts made from it are fitted straight away. If they are stored for several months before being fitted there is a danger that they may become distorted as the wood dries out.

The original type of well-seasoned ash can be difficult to find today, if not impossible. Fortunately, kiln-dried ash can usually be substituted without problems if parts made from it are fitted straight away. If they are stored for several months before being fitted there is a danger that they may become distorted as the wood dries out.

So far as actually cutting out new wooden parts is concerned, a band saw is invaluable, but if such activities are beyond the skills of an amateur restorer, professional help can often be found at a funeral carpenter's works! All the same, when buying wood, make sure it is not twisted and does not have knot holes. Twists can be difficult to eradicate, even for a highly-skilled coffin maker, and knots are a serious cause of weakness.

Old parts that have been taken out of a body should be retained if possible. They can be strengthened with masking tape or pinned to plywood to use as patterns for replacements. In the same way, the old body panels should be retained, even if they are not being repaired. They make the best templates during reconstruction. Such aluminium panels can often provide a heart-breaking sight in that they have survived almost unscathed for fifty years or more, yet be unusable in the restored car because of splits in their wire-beaded edges or corrosion caused by the steel nails used to tack them to the wooden frame.

Steel wings can present a different proposition even though they may be more highly corroded. They are almost invariably made from far thicker material than modern steel components and as a result they can be patched quite successfully. Aluminium panels can be welded, but it is a much more difficult and more skilled process than welding steel. But, at any rate, great care should be taken when removing old steel wings because they may be far more valuable than they appear—and they, too, can provide good patterns if they have to be replaced completely.

One of the main problems of restoring a wooden-framed body is in working out how it was put together in the first place. It was not until a relatively late point in the reconstruction of a Swallow saloon by the monthly magazine, *Practical Classics*, that it was discovered that the frame had been inserted into a readymade aluminium shell rather than the aluminium panels built around the wooden frame. Once this discovery had been made, restoration was much easier! In this case, *Practical Classics* were helped in that Swallows avoided bending ash wherever possible, to save time. Most panels were cut from solid wood, which is much easier today. Steam-bending large pieces of ash for items such as the wheelarches is difficult to say the least and the likelihood of finding anybody who can do it today is remote. *Practical Classics* got over this problem by laminating their wheelarches from sheets of special plywood which bends easily. The end result looked the same when the car was complete and is in no way inferior, justifying such methods.

Special attention is needed when rebuilding ash-framed saloons such as the Swallow.

Once the body had been rebuilt accurately and made strong again, it was then removed from the chassis so that restoration could proceed. The *Practical Classics* methods of making up a frame to locate on the original body mounting holes is an excellent idea which stops the body flexing as it is lifted off.

One of the reasons that the Austin Seven chassis lasts so long in its normal form is that is it not boxed-in. The exposed girders collect a certain amount of road debris, but they do not retain moisture to the extent that is common with boxed sections. As a result, they tend to keep fairly dry and often do not suffer from significant corrosion. Masses of old oil helps, too!

The relatively primitive way in which the chassis was constructed also makes it far easier to repair. It is often simplicity itself to fabricate new steel sections for this chassis.

So far as the rest of the components are concerned, it is chiefly a case of patient dismantling, cleaning, repainting if necessary, and reassembly, or replacement. This is one of the strengths of an Austin Seven when it comes to restoration, or even major maintenance: everything is so small it is relatively easy to lift or remove. It also occupies far less space away from the car while it is being refurbished, which is a tremendous advantage over almost any other form of four-wheeled vintage vehicle.

The steel bodies are far easier to restore, providing they are in substantially sound condition. This is because they are strong enough to be taken off the chassis for a start. Body removal on the Ruby, for instance, is simple once the ten main internal bolts and four external ones have been located. Even then, body removal is not a big job—it needs three people to do it comfortably, but it is not heavy work. Again, the interior is one of the most expensive items to restore, but once the leather is in good condition, it will last almost indefinitely with the proper care. And welding in new metal to replace corroded steel, normally around the bottom of the body and doors, is much simpler than attempting the same work with alloy panels.

Providing the crankshaft is good, engine work is usually confined to only new rings and/or pistons and it is relatively easy to remove the power unit for maintenance: all you need to do is to take off the bonnet, the bonnet brace and horn, radiator, grille, front skirt and starting handle, before disconnecting fuel

Vans can make ideal subjects for restoration.

lines and so on—which is far less than is involved with many other cars.

But if you cannot face such a major job as body restoration, cannot afford it, or your Austin Seven simply does not have one, it is possible to build an excellent reproduction Ulster using a proprietory glass fibre body without changing anything irrevocably. The great advantage of the glass fibre shells is not only that they are cheap, but that they provide an absolutely trouble-free installation, damage is easily repaired, and they are hard to tell apart from the real thing. In fact the only argument against them must be that Austin did not have access to this wonderfully versatile material when the Seven was being built!

Alternatively, there might be an opportunity to construct something really special like this doctor's coupé.

Period type hoods are full of charm.

The Austin Seven engine has to be considered as one of its many strengths.

Mechanical spares are still readily available for the Austin Seven.

A bare chassis awaiting restoration.

The final stages of rebuilding an engine ... running it on a test bed before installation in the chassis.

Originality is of prime importance for concours restoration; all components should be finished as they were when they left the factory, and not over-polished.

X

Common Problems

Austin Sevens have an incredible ability to drag themselves along while suffering from all manner of ailments. Most of them can be associated with plain old age now rather than neglect, but they can be just as numerous nevertheless, and can still be present on the odd example that is found after being stored for years.

Bad starting caused by poor compression is common in some cases. If the car starts only under protest on the handle, worn piston rings or valves are to be suspected. An easy start to the checks for this malady is to disconnect the carburettor feed pipe and turn the engine by hand. Spurts of petrol from the pipe will show that at least the pump is working properly; the carburettor should then be inspected for faults. If it passes with flying colours, check the contact breaker gap and sparking plugs (although a good spark a few inches away from the engine does not necessarily mean that all is well when it is sparking inside). If in doubt, try a new plug.

Further checks should then be made on the tappet clearances, valve gear and cylinder head for possible leaks. If all these items are in good order, practically the only thing left is to check the piston rings—which means taking off the head. Engines suffering from such troubles are likely to be noisy, emitting all sorts of rattles, clunks and thuds. A deep bass rumble may be even worse though. It indicates worn main bearings. An instant way to make sure this is the problem is to press the clutch pedal while the engine is running—although you should never rev an Austin Seven engine more than necessary, even when running without a load, if you want to keep the crank in one piece. Nevertheless, a discreet prod at the clutch will relieve pressure on the ends of the crankshaft, in turn lightening the load on the bearings—which should be enough to stop the rumble.

A high-pitched sound from the dynamo is common, too. The likely cause of this little bit of annoyance is end-float on the dynamo spindle, which can be checked by taking off the cover of the driving pinion, bending the ends of the split pin on the pinion nut to clear the centre of the spindle, and pushing on the end of the spindle with a tommy bar.

Dynamos fitted between 1932 and 1935, for instance, had a fibre washer behind the pinion which caused end-float when it became worn. End-float on

A kaleidoscope of body problems: from the interior of a relatively-sound saloon, to every little fitting needing to be dismantled, to rot in the wooden parts, to corrosion in the steel wings, but frequently a sound floor because it has been soaked in so much oil!

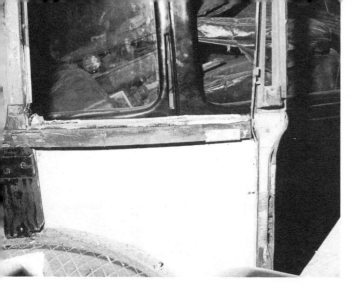

dynamos not fitted with this washer is usually caused by worn bearing races which means that the dynamo has to be stripped for repairs.

Worn timing wheels can set up a tremendous clatter at all sorts of speeds. A quick check while wearing stout working gloves can be made by slackening off the fan belt and holding the fan so that it cannot turn, then with the engine idling, by squeezing the sides of the belt and listening for a reduction in the noise. This is the sort of thing we used to do with Austin Sevens when I worked in a garage as a boy and they were still a common sight on the roads—and I had to make sure that my fingers did not bite onto the pulley!

Clutch slip used to be common, as well, and often could not be cured by adjusting the free movement at the pedal. This invariably meant that the clutch linings were badly worn and this was sometimes accompanied by a metallic whirring which usually meant that the long-suffering Seven had a badly adjusted centre plate. A dry thrust race can make the same sort of noise, but it can be cured by lubrication. Tremors through the clutch pedal usually meant uneven toggle levers, which also made gearchanging difficult.

Brakes pulled one way or the other when they were out of adjustment and juddered when their linings were not chamfered or the rivets were standing proud.

So far as the rest of the car was concerned, visual checks can be enough, bearing in mind that the early chassis are prone to crack just forward of the front cross member, around the rear spring mounting points and around the shock absorber flanges. The points which keep so much corrosion at bay are the joint between the cylinder block and the crankcase, and the joint between the sump and the crankcase. They can let out enough oil on a long motorway run to empty the sump—which I remember accounted for no end of bearing trouble when the M1 motorway was opened in 1959.

Fortunately these joints can be made much more oil tight today by using substances such as Hermatite Instant Gasket; nevertheless, frequent oil checks are a good idea. The three-bearing engines suffer from a notorious problem in that they can wear out their white metal centre bearing in as little as 5000 miles. The likely cause is a slightly misaligned boring made worse by the way the aluminium crankcase flexes. You should expect a higher oil pressure reading on a three-bearing engine of about 8 psi hot, against anything between 1 psi and 5 for the earlier units! Figures taken while the oil is cold can be completely misleading as the indicator is likely to go off its clock. It should return fairly quickly, however, and if it doesn't, suspect a blocked oil jet. You will remember, of course, that this must be cleaned immediately.

If the engine has to be rebuilt, there are a few dodges that I remember. Despite its light weight, it should be stripped of as much as possible while it is still in the car to make handling easier. If you are leaving the gearbox in the car, the rear-end mounting bolts have to be knocked right out because the engine has to clear the splines on the clutch centre plate.

You will also probably find it difficult to get a spanner on the dynamo's front nut. I used to tap it out with a hammer and screwdriver, which worked well

but caused some people to throw up their hands in horror! Alternatively, you can remove the pulley nut and prise the pulley off the tapered shaft.

Once the engine is being stripped, the valves come out quite easily, but they are not quite so easy to replace with their split cone cotters. They will fall down behind the tappets at the drop of a hat, and the easiest way to keep them in place seems to be with plenty of grease.

Taking out the pistons can be tricky because the gudgeon pins are a tight fit and they are clenched in by special screws fitted with locking washers. The screws are 0.25 inch BSF with 0.1875-inch Whitworth heads and need good spanners which fit properly or you'll crush your fingers. The gudgeon pins will be tight enough to need an extractor unless you can drift them out with a rod. But make sure that the pistons and connecting rods are properly supported while you are doing this or you might bend the con-rods.

The oil baffles have to be wiggled out of the crankcase. Before removing the big ends, mark their caps and con-rods so that they can be replaced in the same order. Throw away the split pins (using new ones on re-assembly), unscrew the bolts (again using new ones on re-assembly) and take off the big end caps. You can now lift out the con-rods quite easily.

You are now about halfway through taking the engine to pieces, and the fiddly bits come next. They include removing the front engine cover, the fan driving pulley, the camshaft gear and the starting dog. You have to be careful when you are taking off the camshaft gears because they are made from cast iron and can be cracked if you are too heavy-handed. It is best to use a puller although wooden wedges work well if the gears are kept square while they are driven in from behind.

And the cylinder block and timing gears are very easy to work on because everything is so small.

Before removing the flywheel cover at the other end of the engine, it is essential to trap the mousetrap springs of the clutch release mechanism—they are very powerful. Ideally, you should use a retaining ring to hold down the toggle levers, although it can be done with strong wire. The flywheel is held on by a nut and locking washer. Wooden wedges are ideal here. You jam them between the crankcase and the crankshaft throws, clamp a large adjustable spanner on to the flywheel nut, slip a strong tube over the end and clout it off! The theory behind such clouting is that a small number of sharp blows shift nuts with less likelihood of related damage than sustained pressure with a tommy bar jammed between the rim of the flywheel and the flywheel pit. At any rate, once you've got the nut off, you can either remove the flywheel with a special puller or wedge it off, taking care to keep the wedges in such a position that you can hammer with equal pressure all round the flywheel.

After that it is quite easy to remove the main bearings and crankshaft. The rear housing comes out quite easily by using two 0.3125-inch BSF screws in the holes provided, but the front bearing can be more difficult. The original bearings may have been replaced by dual purpose ball bearings with shim at either end of the races.

To remove the bearings, take off the cover plate and knock the bearings out by tapping on the races from inside the crankcase. The end web of the crankshaft is recessed to allow a drift to be used, but you must be extra careful not to hit the flange casing or it will break. Once the main bearings have been removed, the crankshaft can be wriggled out quite easily.

If the camshaft has to be removed, take off the gear from the oil pump and then the pump. Next take out the camshaft front bearing and the shaft can then be pulled out through the front of the crankcase. The rollers of the centre bearing will drop out leaving the outer track behind.

All the parts stripped from the engine need to be thoroughly checked, of course, but two especially. The first is the crankshaft, which should be measured with a micrometer on the crank pins. Take readings from at least four points around the pins to establish how round they are. Any ovality in excess of 0.005 ins means that the shaft needs to be reground and the big ends remetalled. To check that the big ends have been lapped properly, tighten them up and stand them vertically. They should be able to fall over without stiffness or excessive slack. Then finer checks can be carried out with engineer's blue or boot polish. The main bearings can be checked by washing them in petrol, lubricating them with oil and then spinning them. If the balls are worn, but the tracks are sound, new balls can be fitted but overall wear means total replacement. Make sure that the bearings are a tight fit in their housings and on the crankshaft.

Even the starter ring is easy to handle.

And as for the carburettor...

To eliminate any chance of drag when fitting a relined clutch, make sure that the ends of the toggle levers—the part in which the thrust race presses—are all near enough aligned. They should all be 0.3125 ins from a straight edge held across the face of the flywheel pit. If they vary, they can be corrected by bending them with a tube.

A gauge is needed to fit the centre plate properly. This can be made from a strip of metal drilled to fit on the pit studs with a hole in the middle which locates the splined shaft. Everything is bolted down tight with the gauge in position, which automatically centres the plate. The gauge is then removed...

Timing the engine is quite easy. Remove all the sparking plugs except number one and turn the engine until compression can be felt. Bring the flywheel mark (1/4 seen through the top of the clutch pit) to top centre, which brings number one piston to the top of its stroke. Now move the flywheel back 1.875 ins and turn the distributor casing until the contacts are just beginning to open with the rotor arm pointing to the number one plug segment. The spark is then timed for all cylinders and final adjustment can be left until the car is on the road.

You can check the gearbox for wear by taking off the top and examining the gate and selector forks. You need to remove the front cover to examine the thrust bearing and the first bearing of the input shaft. Then swill out the box with petrol watching carefully for metal dust or fragments. If the gearbox passes this test, refill it with engine oil and it is likely to run sweetly for years. Rear axles are similarly tough.

To test the brakes properly, the procedure is similar with all Austin Sevens. Taking the later cars as an example, depress the foot pedal sufficiently to apply the brakes, but not hard enough to lock the wheels. Then wedge the pedal in place. Jack the car up and twist each wheel in turn, judging the differences in resistance. The whole lot should then be adjusted to allow an inch or so of free travel at the pedal before the brakes are fully applied, by means of the wing nuts under the car. Avoid twisting the cables when making the rear individual adjustments. If, despite your best efforts, you find that you cannot balance the whole set-up with one or more wheels still moving easily, the brakes need re-lining.

First take off the wheel or wheels, then the brake drums with the help of a hub extractor. The outer portions of the front hubs are covered by a cap which must be removed, followed by the oiling plug which will otherwise foul the bearing when you withdraw the hub. Next, remove the axle nut and replace the outer portion of the hub, fixing it to the rear part with the wheel nuts. Before using the extractor, get it well screwed down on the hubs. If you cannot shift it with a big spanner, attach an equally large adjustable to it with the length of tubing for extra leverage. And if that doesn't work, stand on the end and gently bounce up and down! You can now draw off the complete hub with the bearing and packing, leaving access to the brake shoes. The rear hubs also include a bearing unit which must be removed. If you find that the front cable has stretched upon refitting, I gather that you can still get cable crimpers from some Halford's cycle shops for use in an emergency.

While the wheels are off the ground, check the king pins. If they are slack, you will need an extractor to get them out, but you must replace the bushes at the same time as they are serviced and you will need a special reamer to finish the job.

To take up end-play in the steering column, screw the outer column into, or out of, the steering box. Loosen the nut which tightens the outer column to the instrument board. Then unscrew the locking peg and clamping bolt at the bottom of the column and turn the sleeve until the play is taken up. Don't overdo it, or you will end up with stiff steering.

When you have adjusted the sleeves, the locking peg must be made to enter one of the sleeve slots. If you have clearance between the worm and the worm wheel, first slacken the three nuts holding the cover to the worm casing and then turn the adjusting screw to draw the cover in the direction of the worm. The aim should be freedom of steering without end-play or backlash.

And finally, make sure that you have 0.125 ins of toe-in or you'll crucify your front tyres. If it needs adjustment, disconnect the cross tube lever from the nearside swivel axle. This frees the steering cross tube for adjustment on the nearside. You then have to slacken off the clamping bolt of the steering arm jaw and screw the jaw on or off the tube as necessary to correct the toe-in.

But all the time you are having fun like this, remember that the glory of an old car like an Austin Seven is that you can take it all to pieces, quite unlike modern machinery. What will enthusiasts do in sixty years' time when they try to repair one of today's cars full of sophisticated electronic contraptions which by then will have been long out of production?

Chassis work is equally straightforward.

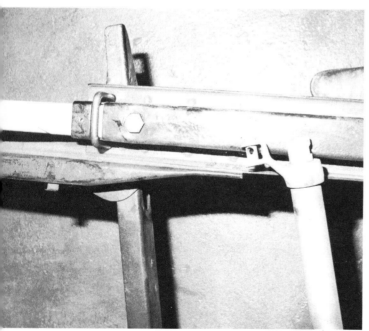

XI

The Interchangeability of Spare Parts

Austin Sevens can be built from an almost endless supply of different parts, either second hand or remanufactured, the interchangeability rate is so high. Just which component can be linked to another is largely a matter of how original an owner wants to keep a car. An Ulster can be built around the frame of a 1931 tourer, for instance, which is virtually the same except for having a different torque tube ball joint. The suspension for the 'new' Ulster can then be taken from a Nippy, and so on. But now that originality is all the rage in old car circles, it is wise to stick to specific age groups when it comes to selecting spare parts for an Austin Seven, particularly if value is of paramount importance. Within these bounds, spares are largely the same; parts from another age group will often fit, or can be adapted, but they will not necessarily be as near original as matters to the purists.

All magneto engines built between 1923 and 1928 had the same crankcase, with the fittings varying only in detail between, chiefly, cars with a fan and without one. In the same way, the coil ignition engines made between 1928 and 1932 used basically the same crankcase and fittings, although changes were made to the rear main bearing housing and retaining plate in 1929. The crankcases made between 1932 and 1936 had the same fittings, although the engine mountings were changed in 1933, and the starting handle shaft in 1932 and 1934. For the purposes of such interchangeability, all three-bearing engines made from 1936 to 1939 had basically the same crankcase and fittings, and you can fit the same oil pump to any engine.

Camshafts, on the other hand, changed frequently, with new ones in 1923, 1924, 1928, 1932 and 1936, although some of the ancilliaries can be swopped around.

Magneto engine crankshafts and their associated parts made between 1923 and 1928 are all the same unless they did not need a fan. The coil ignition engine crankshafts and fittings were unaltered between 1928 and 1930, and 1930 and 1936 save for new front bearings in 1933. The three-bearing cranks were also the same except for a change of bearing size in 1937.

So far as cylinder blocks are concerned, the magneto engine versions are all the same with the coil editions showing only the odd change to valvegear in 1934

Engine parts are among the most interchangeable between models.

and 1935 and to the studs in 1936. Cylinder heads can be swopped around with wild abandon, the chief changes only in 1928 and 1936. Major manifold changes took place only in 1932, and exhaust systems are dependent only on the car's wheelbase unless it is a sports model.

Petrol pumps are split into two types, the M from 1932 to 1934 and the T to 1939. Flywheels, clutches and associated fittings are all the same between 1923 and 1932; 1933 and 1936, 1936 and 1938 (the Newton-Bennett type) and 1938 and 1939 (Borg and Beck).

The three-speed gearboxes are basically the same, with a change of third motion shaft in 1926, casing in 1927, covers, gate, gaskets and numerous small parts in 1929. The crash first and second gearboxes made between 1933 and 1934 are identical, as are the crash first boxes of 1934 to 1939, apart from a cover change in 1937.

The four-speed gearbox is only 0.75 ins longer than the three-speed and can be substituted providing a variety of other modifications are carried out. The output spider of the three-speed gearbox is part of the third motion shaft and cannot be altered easily, but the equivalent part of the four-speed gearbox is splined on and the 1933–4 spider can be changed for the later circular flanged type as used on the needle-roller shaft.

Propeller shafts fitted between 1923 and 1931 are similar except for their long or short-wheelbase length to those used between 1931 and 1933, when the Hardy Spicer type was introduced.

Rear axles, on the other hand, are a law unto themselves! Noted Austin Seven expert Jack French summed it all up in a lecture to the 750 MC, related in their excellent publication, the *Austin Seven Companion*:

'The shortage of bits and pieces during and after the war produced some astonishing wangles and "conversions," the majority of which are better forgotten; the following changes, however, are quite permissable and help to enhance the versatility of the Seven.

'The 1929 crown wheel and pinion can go into earlier casings providing the carrier is also changed. So far as the screw-in torque tube axle is concerned, you can change the entire torque tube assembly for any of the later types. This enables you to use any pinion which has the bearing-retaining thread.

'The Ulster 5.67 can be used only with its own special casing, being too large to fit into the others. On large models, from 1931 onwards, there is comparatively easy interchangeability. Pinions intended for post 1934 models with a roller race have a shoulder on 1.125 in diameter next to the teeth. If you are fitting one of these to an earlier axle, there are three ways of doing it:

'One: Use a light type of ball race fitting onto the shoulder, and a larger diameter distance piece between the races. The outside diameter of the ball race will be the same as that of the old one. The snag is that the light race will be even less strong than the old one, so don't do this if your car is going to be driven hard.

'Two: Convert the pinion to the earlier pattern by grinding off the shoulder. This is perhaps the best compromise if facilities are available; note that perfect concentricity is essential.

'Three: convert the banjo casing to the roller race type. This involves the fitting of two extra parts, a peg to stop the outer ring of the race from wandering off into the cogwheel, and a distance piece to stop it moving forward.

'If you are fitting a ball race type crown and pinion into a roller race casing, you can do three things:

'Make a steel sleeve to fit onto the pinion so that you can still use the roller race; use the appropriate ball race, throwing away the distance piece and making sure that the race does not foul the peg; or use a heavier type of roller race, the bore and outside diameter of which are such that it will fit both the pinion and the casing. It will be thicker than the original, so you must take an appropriate amount off the distance pieces which fit between the races.'

Alternatively, you can make up your own ratios by the Chapman method with the aid of Bluebell metal polish, providing you don't mind sacrificing a set of bearings in the process.

But with more original exchanges in mind, all front axles were the same from 1924 to 1936 in either touring or sports adaptations, and from 1936 to 1939. The steering boxes occupied similar periods of production from 1923 to 1936 with only the column changing in 1929, and from 1936 to 1939. Hubs were largely the same on all Austin Sevens save for a change from a taper bore to parallel bore in 1926.

A wide variety of wheels and tyres were fitted: 19-inch from 1925 to 1934

Wheel braces as original.

Exhaust systems featured few variables.

And they nearly all swept up over the rear axle.

Wheels can frequently be swopped around with merry abandon.

And chassis can be adapted to carry a wide variety of bodywork.

But little details such as tread plates can be special to just one model.

Interchangeable ... but only just, and very, very rare: a multi-stud supercharged Seven engine.

and 17-inch from 1935 with 18-inch in specialised adaptations. Brakes changed with the wheels and the taper bearings in 1926 with the shoes going up from 1 in to 1.25 ins in 1932 and to Girling-type operation in 1936. Spring change dates were 1926, 1931 and 1934 with special versions for sports models and vans. Rear shock absorbers had long arms before 1934 and short ones after, and front ones short bolts before 1930 and long ones after.

Distributors are all basically the same, pre 1934 or post 1934, the CAV dynamo fitted from 1923 to 1928 having a change of bearings, Woodruff key and driving gear in 1925, followed by the CAV/Lucas type from 1928 to 1931, and Lucas between 1932 and 1935 before it was uprated. Starter motors had three periods: from 1923 to 1929; 1929 to 1932 and 1932 to 1939, and, last but not least, when it comes to looking authentic: the wiring loom had cotton braiding before 1936, when it was changed to PVC.

XII

The Man Behind the Austin Seven

Repeated investigations have revealed that there was really only one man behind the Austin Seven, with all others playing only incidental parts. He was born plain Herbert Austin, son of a farmer called Giles from Great Missenden, Bucks, in 1866, and could be said to come of yeoman stock. Like many farming families, the Austins fell on hard times in the late nineteenth century and Giles had to take a job as a farm bailiff in the north of England. As a result he was able to offer only a bleak future for Herbert as his son attended Rotherham Grammar School in Yorkshire. But Herbert was a bright boy and uncommonly good at technical drawing and making mechanical things work. Apprenticeships in architecture and on the railways did not prove fruitful, however, so that when he was sixteen, he decided to go to the promised land, Australia, with an uncle.

Once in Australia, Austin found his forte with the Wolseley sheep shearing company, making their mechanical clippers work better. Even then he had what amounted to a mania for making mechanical things reliable and longer lasting. It is easy to compare the dedication he displayed in this field with that of another engineer, his contemporary, Frederick Royce, whose perfectionism gained such a great reputation for Rolls-Royce.

When viewed from another angle, Austin could be said to be pig-headed: once he had made up his mind about what course to follow, nothing could deflect him. Two years after marrying a Scots-Australian girl called Helen Dron, while earning a decent wage of £3.50 a week, he decided to sell up everything and gamble on returning to his family in Birmingham. Fortunately the gamble paid off and within four years of his return he was made manager of the British arm of Wolseley. All things mechanical fascinated him and whenever he thought up a way of improving anything, he patented it in the manner of the times.

But he couldn't patent his first motor car, built among the sheep clipping machines in 1898, because it was almost a straight copy of a French Bollee tri-car. Like Royce, Austin did not necessarily invent anything, he just made it work a lot better. But pig-headed or not, he inspired loyalty among many people, and soon he was joined at Wolseley by his brother, Harry, who—with several other close associates—would work with him for the rest of his life.

Gradually the new-fangled cars became all important to Wolseley, with Austin firmly in charge and refusing to be swayed from the horizontal engine. He was also convinced that racing improved the breed and drove one of his cars in the 1903 Paris–Madrid race. But when the racing cars were less than successful in 1905, the Wolseley directors lost their enthusiasm for racing, and Austin decided the time had come to set up on his own.

He managed to scrape together enough money to buy a derelict factory at Longbridge, near Birmingham, in 1905, with his brother, Harry, Bob Hewitt as his private secretary and two other recruits from Wolseley: designers Joey Hancock and A.V. Davidge.

Money was tight, but as veteran journalist Rodney Walkerley recalled in *Thoroughbred and Classic Cars* in 1978, Austin did not mind his bare, cobwebbed, little office (in fact he kept it for the rest of his life). By 1908, he was producing seventeen different models which had quickly gained a reputation for being comfortable and well-made—plus a grand prix car! The sombre figure of Herbert Austin bred sturdy and dependable stock, but still had an eye for a thoroughbred racer. The following year he made his first Seven to fulfil one of the dreams which had caused him to leave Australia: he would not budge from the conviction that the world needed a cheap, strong, small, car. He had seen that very need for dependable, economical, transport as he toured the outback.

It is said that Austin was at his most creative while enjoying his only pursuit outside the motor car: long solitary cycle rides. But he also had a great love for classical music, although he worked hard and for so many hours that he had little time to attend concerts. It was typical of Austin, that when faced with such frustration, work came first: but he found a way of enjoying his music in the background by starting one of the first comprehensive record collections. With classical strains echoing around him, he worked happily at his drawing board in the billiards room of his home, Lickey Grange, within earshot of Longbridge.

By 1912, when the cycle-maker, William Morris, was building his first light car, Austin was making 1,000 a year. And during the war his energetic contribution gained him a knighthood in 1917—although at some expense to his Austin Motor Company which languished in the doldrums during the post-war depression. Sir Herbert continued to concentrate on his 12-hp medium-priced car, but despite the support of his many friends, by 1921 he found himself tottering on the verge of bankruptcy. The outlook was grim when a former naval officer, Commander C.R. Engelbach, took over the running of his company as Official Receiver.

Sir Herbert might have had a naval man at the helm, but he was still master. He stuck to his guns and virtually locked a young assistant, Stanley Edge, in his billiards room to work day and night on the small car which had been on his mind since the turn of the century. Sir Herbert was seen for most of the day to be running his business from the works. But when he left, he spent half the night in the billiards room, discussing progress on the small car with Edge. At other times, when he was able to escape from the works, such as on train journeys, he sketched plans for the car in a notebook, leaving Edge to turn the blueprints into reality. Without a doubt, Edge's input was tremendous, but there must be little doubt that Austin was the major influence. As Walkerley recalled:

'Austin was a dynamo. No one looked at clocks when he was at work—and nobody cared.

'Herbert was a fairly short man. As time went on he became pleasantly portly, with balding head and a small moustache. He always wore a bowler hat and stiff white collars. Later, about the time of his Baronetcy in 1936, he took to the black homburg hat popularised by Anthony Eden. He neither drank nor smoked and immediately distrusted those who did, at least in his works. It was inevitable his workforce called him "Pa," for he looked the part of the stern disciplinarian but kind-hearted *pater familias* of the Edwardians. It caused no surprise to see "Pa" in his shirt sleeves, at a machine, showing a nervous beginner how to do the job properly, carefully and quickly. After all, there was no operation Herbert could not do as he wanted it done.'

As we know, Edge's main contribution, apart from hours of dedicated work, to the Austin Seven design was in the engine department. He was born at Old Hill, Staffs, in 1903, to a reasonably well-off family, his mother being a teacher and his father a legal clerk. As a result he had a good education at private school, followed by Halesowen Grammar School, where he showed an especial aptitude for technical drawing, virtually teaching himself! He was also a voracious reader with a wonderful memory, absorbing masses of technical data. In 1916 he started work for Austins and that led to a job in the drawing office in 1917—when he was still only fourteen. Following work on aircraft design, Edge transferred to cars in 1918 under Hancock. As the young man had few responsibilities at the age of seventeen and a very diplomatic manner, he was a natural choice to assist Sir Herbert at Lickey Grange. Edge is quick to point out, however, that he was actually eighteen by the time he started drawing the Austin Seven.

One of his main abilities was also to be very persuasive, supporting his theories with well-chosen facts, neatly presented. Even as work was progressing on the Seven, Sir Herbert, who was far less gruff and more fatherly once he was away from the works, still wanted a horizontal engine because it gave a lower centre of gravity—despite being unable to produce an effective one since he left Wolseley! However, Edge was a strong student of engine design, consuming every written word on the subject and duly presented Sir Herbert with a comprehensive typewritten list of specifications that showed the trend among small Continental cars was towards the vertical four-cylinder unit. Austin then followed this theory, which was quite easy in any case because the Austin Seven engine then amounted in many ways to a scaled-down version of what he was already producing!

Once the Austin Seven design work was finished, however, and Edge had returned to the mainstream of Austin design office work, everything else seemed an anti-climax. He eventually left in 1925 to pursue a distinguished career in hydraulics engineering that was to continue into the 1980s.

Charles Goodacre recalled well the reception accorded to the Seven in 1922 during an interview with Philip Turner in *Motor* in 1973:

> 'People said it was stupid and nobody would buy such a silly car. But it was a properly designed and properly engineered motor car, which was not true of many of the light cars of that era, such as the GN, the AV Monocar, and such like. These weren't motor cars, they were a cross between poor aviation and henhouse engineering. The Austin Seven was a real motor car. It looked like a scaled-down Austin 20 or 12, it was reliable, it was a very nice little car to drive, and it had very good roadability. When Sir Herbert scheduled production at 300 a week, people said he was crazy and wouldn't sell 50 a week. But soon he had to go up to 500 a week. When people laughed at his Austin Seven, his immediate reaction was to show what he could do by racing it.'

As Edge was an avid reader of books on engine design, Sir Herbert was an equally avid student of other people's success. Practically the only picture he hung on the walls of his office at Longbridge was that of a Model T Ford, at that time the world's most popular car. His Austin 20 was a British equivalent, and the 12 a scaled-down version—although the Seven was to take on the Model T's mantle in Britain, which needed a smaller car. Austin's production methods bore a marked resemblance to those of Ford, too.

His production philosophy was that you made as many of the car's components yourself, so that any profit came back to you, rather than going out to some accessory firm. Although Sir Herbert was not seen as being a financial wizard, he was certainly shrewd in a countryman-like way. He bitterly regretted having had to allow his Austin Motor Company to go public, but still managed to wring an agreement out of the directors that he should be paid 2 guineas per car produced—so that Austin Seven production made him a very wealthy man with its many patented features.

By 1925 the Austin Motor Company was out of the red and Sir Herbert was well on the way to amassing a personal fortune, with Ernest Payton—who had very good connections in the City of London—as his financial director. With Commander Engelbach, the former receiver who had become works manager, these three men ran the company in a very personal manner, almost as a feudal empire. Goodacre remembers: 'The Austin company was popularly known as the old umbrella, for if you worked for it you could never, ever, be fired, unless you robbed the till.'

Nevertheless, Sir Herbert proposed a merger with his rival, Morris, in 1925 that was turned down by Morris, who had an equally strong character and viewed Austin with great suspicion. The two men clashed again in 1927 when Wolseley—once Britain's biggest motor manufacturer—was ailing and up for sale. Whatever Austin offered, Morris bid more and more. Austin was dogged, but eventually gave up and the Morris Minor followed with Wolseley's overhead camshaft engine that found its way into the all-conquering M.Gs. By that time, in the early 1930s, Austin was making a lot of money and he eventually authorised an all-out racing car to beat the M.G. menace—the twin cam Seven.

He had lost his only son, Vernon, to a sniper's bullet at the Somme in 1915, and allowed Arthur Waite, an Australian who had married his vivacious daughter, Irene, to pursue whatever path appealed to him within the Austin Motor Company. Waite had all the right ideas, but never seemed to be blessed with the right amount of success. As Goodacre recalled, Waite was initially taken with racing and had the first supercharged Austin Seven built for himself at great expense, with a modified version of the previous season's works racer as a back-up car for a second driver. Waite was a shrewd judge of the 'old man's' character, as Goodacre remembered:

'When the question of a driver for the second car was raised by Sir Herbert, Waite said they had better let Alf Depper, the racing shop foreman, have a go. It was the old man's principle that if you built racing cars and they were any good then works drivers should be able to win with them. After 1926, Sir Herbert worked on the principle that if you had 250 apprentices at the factory and you could not find two or three enthusiastic young men who were good enough drivers to win races with the cars, then the cars were no good. He liked to employ works drivers because you could control them and he didn't have to pay them any money. He paid them a bonus only if they were successful and any prize money came to the company. Then, of course, with all due respect, these young apprentices were expendable, because they had no dependent relatives, no children to look after or wives or anything like that. So you insured their lives for £10,000 and that was it...

'Moreover this policy of employing works drivers meant that if a car was successful with a works driver it raised the morale of the whole company because it had all been done in house.'

Nevertheless, Sir Herbert could be impressed by people he could not buy. As R.J. Wyatt recounted in his excellent book, *The Austin Seven*, Gordon England, one of Britain's first test pilots, had his ankle in plaster when he went to see Sir Herbert to try to persuade him to race the Austin Seven in 1922. Sir Herbert sounded hardly encouraging to England, already an established racing driver, when he greeted him with the words: 'What the hell do you want to see me about?' England told him that Austin's new car was still not taken seriously, even by his own staff, and that the only way to get it launched properly would be to establish it as a racing car, and that he, Gordon England, was the man to do it. Looking at England's ankle, Sir Herbert replied: 'You'd make a bloody fine racing driver!' But the ice was broken and England got his first car free of charge before his leg was out of plaster. You could almost hear old farmer Giles talking...

Gordon England applied aircraft standards of preparation to his racing cars and benefited accordingly, whereas Waite had to take pot luck with whatever mechanics were provided by the works—and they were not always enthusiastic. Gordon England's coachbuilding firm also leaped ahead by jumps and bounds because he was an autocratic boss who insisted on everything being done exactly right and no slacking. He was able to build bodies for all manner of cars without having the distraction of having to worry about developing running gear. Even Sir Herbert had to follow suit, such was the success of his Austin Seven saloon.

But Sir Herbert resolved to keep a firmer grip on racing activities when he heard good reports of Tom Murray Jamieson's activities. Goodacre recalled:

'He was a young graduate of Battersea Polytechnic who had been engaged by Amherst Villiers to work on a project for supercharging a 40/50 hp Rolls-Royce by mounting a supercharged Austin Seven engine on the running board solely to drive a much bigger supercharger, which in turn supercharged the Rolls-Royce engine. The whole project never came to anything, but the Austin Seven engine and its special blower were installed in an Ulster and it went very well.

'Villiers then sold Sir Herbert the idea of considerably increasing the power of their racing engines by using this supercharger. Austin asked for the engine and supercharger to be sent to Longbridge and I was given the job of testing it. As far as I can recall, it produced about the same power as the engine with a Cozette blower, an off-the-shelf unit which had to be bought from a French company...'

Further tests with methanol fuel were so promising that Austin, scenting the possibility of making his own supercharger, made a deal with Villiers, and, according to Goodacre:

'Took Jamieson and set him up in a little drawing office on his own. To start with he produced some modifications to the side valve engine which became quite well known, but his success was very limited because the cylinder block of the side valve engine was the very devil owing to thermodynamic problems ... our short-tail single seaters, known as the Rubber Ducks, were being swamped by the M.G. competition ... and it was obvious that the lemon had been squeezed dry so far as the side valve engine was concerned.

'Sir Herbert used to walk about 10 miles a day through his factory. He knew everyone and was involved in many things in the factory including the testing of all new experimental cars. He came into the racing shop one evening as usual and asked me what I thought could be done to deal with the M.G.s. I said there was only one thing for it. He had to face the necessity of producing a new racing engine.

'No doubt many people gave him the same advice, for he called Jamieson into his office and instructed him to design and build within 18 months a world-beating 750 cc engine. Jamieson was given a clean sheet of paper and told this is the requirement, meet it. The ridiculous sum of

The Austin Seven team for the 1929 Tourist Trophy race.

1. GORDON ENGLAND
2. J.D.BARNES
3. GUNNAR POPPE
4. A.FRAZER NASH
5. F.S.BARNES
6. G.E.COLDICUTT
7. S.V.HOLBROOK

£10,000, as I recall, was set aside in the company's budget for the production of the first car....

'Jamieson was given the complete run of any facilities that the company had in the factory, which by then covered roughly 36 acres and employed 23,000 people.

'Austin went off to America and Jamieson settled down to the job of designing the new racing engine. It was a very secret job, but as I recall, it was a mid-engined affair. The driver sat in front of the engine in a semi-prone position and there was a subsidiary fuel tank between the driver and the engine. The beam type front axle passed under the driver's knees and de Dion suspension was used at the rear. Monocoque construction was used for the hull and sponsons between the 20-inch wheels housed the main fuel tanks and the surface radiators, with additional cooling surfaces in the nose between two adjustable wings. There was also a rear fin. The engine was very similar to the one used in the twin cam cars, but was laid down with two-stage supercharging and fuel injection. Two plugs per cylinder and two valves per cylinder were other features. The engine was really inspired by Ricardo's Vauxhall TT engine of which Jamieson had gained some experience when he worked with Villiers and by the Lory-designed Delage engine of which Jamieson had some drawings. These two engines were responsible for the use of the 100-degree valve angle, with the biggest valves possible. The car would have been about 24 ins high with a dry weight of 7 cwt and with the engine producing 160 bhp at 12,000 rpm. The designed maximum speed of the car was 165 mph...

'When Lord Austin returned from overseas, the dust sheets were removed and he asked Jamieson to tell him all about it. Jamieson went through the whole thing—it took him about 25 minutes—and Lord Austin listened very patiently, then said: "I congratulate you on a very forward thinking piece of design but I am sorry Jamieson, I'm not having it. It is not for me. It is a lethal device to win races, not a car. If I put any of my young men into that and they crash, it will kill them."

'Jamieson started to argue the point, but Austin was adamant. He said: "I know it's a disappointment to you, but I'll come up into your office this evening and show you what I want. An orthodox car with the engine in front of the driver."

'Jamieson, therefore designed the twin overhead camshaft Austin along orthodox lines. In my opinion the performance of the engine was limited by a fundamental mistake, the 100-degree valve angle, that meant you couldn't get a high enough compression ratio.

'Unfortunately Jamieson insisted on doing all the initial test driving himself at Donington. He was a very good driver, but not a true racing driver and therefore did not flog the car hard enough to clear up its faults. It was a very forward thinking car and the engine was promising, but initially it was very unreliable. Unfortunately before the car got going properly Jamieson was in political difficulties with the company, for there were very many people who wanted to stop the project.

'Jamieson became one of the few people to be sacked by Austin and joined the ERA racing car firm, only to die tragically while spectating at Brooklands soon after. In Goodacre's opinion he was 20 years' ahead of his time, but it was nearer 30 when Colin Chapman's Lotus 25 became the world's first monocoque grand prix car to a similar configuration to this stillborn design.

'Jamieson was a brilliant engineer, but like many brilliant engineers he was very dogmatic,' said Goodacre. 'But he was one of the nicest gentlemen you could ever wish to meet. They didn't come any better. Unfortunately he had no political sense whatever, and in my opinion he was murdered by a bunch of politicians at Longbridge—and I don't care who knows it.'

By this time, in 1936, Goodacre had left Austin to work for one of their distributors, but he was recalled by Lord Austin in 1937, who told him he had 'ploughed a very lone furrow' on the racing programme, which had cost the company £50,000. Goodacre was given six weeks to make the cars successful and did so with few modifications. He was almost a second Gordon England.

Like Morris, Austin became a philanthropist in his later years, although not on the same scale. He supported Birmingham hospitals and Lord Rutherford's 'atom factory' at Cambridge, some said as an alternative to Morris's activities at Oxford. When he became a governor of the rebuilt theatre at Stratford-upon-Avon, typically he redesigned the seating to make it more comfortable. Inevitably, Longbridge was bombed as it went over to munitions again in 1940. Six of Sir Herbert's workers were killed and he caught pneumonia attending their funeral.

He died aged 75 in 1941, still the boss. He was mourned by 20,000 workers, his wife—who had maintained a very happy and well-run almost feudal, home—two daughters and one grandson. They all called him Pa—the man who made the Austin Seven almost by himself.

Sir Herbert Austin used his attractive daughters Irene, left, and Zeta, right, to help promote the Seven in its early years.

XIII

The Austin Seven Clubs

Austin Seven owners are lucky in that they have a wide variety of clubs to cater for their interests—more than 30 major ones throughout the world. They organise all the usual meetings—mostly monthly—and offer help with technical information, spares, and publish monthly magazines and newsletters as well as running all manner of social events such as film shows, dinners, dances, barbecues and in Britain particularly, pub meetings. For more information on these clubs you can contact them through the Austin Seven Clubs' Association, the secretary of which is Robin Newman, of Dixton Cottage, Monmouth, Gwent, Wales NP5 3SJ.

There are also two clubs in particular which cater specifically for competition-minded owners, the 750 Motor Club and the Vintage Sports-Car Club.

From its formation in 1939, the 750 MC became a non-profit making company in 1955 organising monthly meetings all over Britain which usually took the form of film shows or talks. The club organises more than 50 low-cost motor sporting events each year as well as the National Birkett Six-Hour Relay. Although it now caters for the owners of other motor vehicles, it still has a substantial Austin Seven section which operates a spares and advice service and organises trials. The club's general secretary is Dave Bradley, of 16 Woodstock Road, Witney, Oxon, England OX8 6DT.

The Vintage Sports-Car Club was founded in 1934 to run events and cater for the owners of cars that were more than five years old on 1 January 1935. By 1936, it had been agreed that only cars made before 1931 were vintage, a decision prompted by the fact that after 1930 mass production had generally got into its stride.

Competitions were organised ranging from trials, through treasure hunts to speed trials and races before the VSCC became one of the first clubs to organise speed events after the war—at Elstree in 1946 and Gransden Lodge in 1947. The VSCC was also the first club to run a meeting at Silverstone in April 1949. As the years went on, the club's attitude to the 1931 deadline mollified and now all Austin Seven sports cars are allowed to enter their invariably over-subscribed events.

Symbol of the Seven ... the Bristol Club's logo.

The secretary, Peter Hull, can be contacted at the VSCC, 121 Russell Road, Newbury, Berks, England RG14 5JX.

Austin Sevens climb the second highest pass in Wales on a club run.

Line-up at a club meeting.

Austineers delight in getting off the road where no modern vehicle dare tread ... just for a natter.

And they love a sing-song in the evening!

Camping is one of the favourite pastimes of Austin Seven club members.

The leaving of the campsite can be a lot of fun ... when there is always a helping hand.

And then there's always another day for another run ...

212

And lots of interesting cars to exhibit.

Then its all hands on deck to pre-
pare for the run home.

Part of the line-up of Austin Sevens
at their Diamond Jubilee at Crof-
ton Park in 1982.

The mystery 1923 doctor's coupé popped up at a club meeting alongside a '28 tourer.

There's always a home for an Austin Seven...

Austin Sevens on parade ... at Brands Hatch's Festival of Yester-year in 1984.

XIV
Your Austin Seven Logbook

Austin Seven tourer

Approximately 42,500 made from 1922 plus approximately 13,000 bare chassis sold from 1925.

Engine

Four cylinders, in-line, side valve CUBIC CAPACITY 696 cc; BORE AND STROKE 50 mm × 85 mm; MAX POWER 10 bhp at 2400 rpm; (from March 1923) CUBIC CAPACITY 747 cc; BORE AND STROKE 56 mm × 76 mm.

Chassis

WEIGHT 800 lb; dimensions: WHEELBASE 6 ft 3 ins; FRONT TRACK 3 ft 4 ins; REAR TRACK 3 ft 4 ins; LENGTH 9 ft 1 in; WIDTH 3 ft 10 ins; HEIGHT (hood erect) 4 ft 10 ins; FRONT SUSPENSION live axle, half-elliptic transverse spring, leading links; REAR SUSPENSION live axle, quarter-elliptic springs, torque tube; BRAKES drum all round; gearing (overall) 4.5:1, 8, 14.5; TYRES AND WHEELS 26 ins × 3 ins (from March 1925) TYRES AND WHEELS 26 ins × 3.5 ins (from 1931 WEIGHT 1000 lb, WHEELBASE 6 ft 9 ins; REAR TRACK 3 ft 7 ins; OVERALL GEARING 5.25, 9.65, 17.1 (from September 1932) OVERALL GEARING 5.25, 9.05, 14.4, 23.3 (from 1934) WHEELS AND TYRES 17 ins × 4.00 ins (from June 1936) ENGINE 16.5 bhp at 3400 rpm.

Austin Seven saloon

Approximately 232,500 made from 1926; approximately 20,000 vans made from October 1923.
As tourer except LENGTH 9 ft 3 ins, WEIGHT 1100 lb (from 1931) 1200 lb; (from October 1937) engine CUBIC CAPACITY 900 cc, BORE AND STROKE 56.77 mm × 88.9 mm, MAX POWER 24 bhp at 4000 rpm; WEIGHT 1650 lb.

Austin Seven sports

Approximately 7000 made from January 1924.

As tourer except length 10 ft 4 ins; (from 1929–31) engine: non-supercharged MAX POWER 24 bhp at 5000 rpm; supercharged MAX POWER 33 bhp at 5000 rpm, overall GEAR RATIOS 4.9, 7, 12.5, WHEELS AND TYRES 3.90 ins × 18 ins (from 1933) engine MAX POWER 23 bhp at 4800 rpm, overall GEARING 5.625, 8.38, 13.33, 21.32 (from 1934) optional 28 bhp engine, or 12 bhp.

Index

Picture Acknowledgements

The Author is grateful to the following organisations and photographers for allowing their pictures to be used.

British Motor Industry Heritage Trust 1, 2, 3 Top, 5 Bottom, 6 Top, 10, 14 Top, 15, 16, 17, 18, 19 Top & Bottom, 20, 23, 24 Top & Bottom, 25 Top, 26 Top, 27, 28 Top & Bottom, 29, 30 Top & Bottom, 31, 32 Top & Bottom, 33, 34, 37 Top, 38 Top, 40, 43 Top, 46, 52, 53 Bottom, 55 Top Centre Bottom, 56, 58, 59 Top Right Centre Bottom, 60 Top, Centre Left and Bottom, 61, 63 Top, 82 Top, 85 Top, 92 Top & Bottom, 112, 114 Top & Bottom, 116, 117 Top & Bottom, 123 Top & Bottom, 124, 128, 129, 130, 131, 132, 134, 135, 136, 205, 207.

Bruce, Neill Cover, Colour Plates 2, 3, 5, 6, 7. Pages 5 Top, 38 Bottom, 44, 51 Bottom, 54 Bottom, 63 Bottom, 69 Right, 83, 84 Top, 118, 147 Centre, 151 Top Centre & Bottom, 135 Bottom, 154 Top Left and Right, 173 Top Left & Right, 190 Top Left & Right, 198, 212 Top, 214 Bottom.

Haynes, John H. 166, 169, 170, 171.

Hilton Press Services, Colour Plates 1, 4, 8, 9, 10, 11, 12, 13, 14, 15, 16, 17, 18, 19, 20, 21, 22, 23, 24, 25, 26. Pages 3 Bottom, 6 Bottom, 7, 11, 12, 13, 14 Bottom, 25 Bottom, 26 Bottom, 35, 37 Bottom Left & Right, 41, 42 Top & Bottom, 43 Bottom, 45 Top, Bottom Left and Right, 51 Top, 53 Top, 54 Top, 57 Top, Centre & Bottom, 59 Top Left, 60 Centre Right, 65 Top & Bottom, 67, 68, 69 Left, 72 Top, Bottom Left & Right, 73 Top, Bottom Left & Right, 74, 75 Top & Bottom, 77 Top Left & Right, Bottom, 78 Top, Bottom Left & Right, 79 Top & Bottom, 80, 82 Bottom Left & Right, 84 Bottom, 85 Bottom, 94 Top & Bottom, 97 Top, Bottom Left & Right, 100 Left & Right, 103, 105, 144 Top & Bottom, 145 Top, Bottom Left & Right, 146 Top Left & Right, Centre & Bottom, 147 Bottom, 148 Top Left & Right, Bottom, 149 Top Left & Right, Centre & Bottom, 150 Top & Bottom, 152 Top Left & Right, Centre & Bottom, 153 Top & Centre, 154 Centre & Bottom, 158 Top Centre & Bottom, 159 Top Left & Right, Centre, Bottom Left & Right, 162 Top Left & Right, Centre & Bottom, 161 Top & Bottom, 162 Top Left & Right Bottom, 163 Top Left & Right, Bottom, 164 Top Left & Right, Bottom, 165 Top, Centre & Bottom, 172 Top & Bottom, 173 Centre & Bottom, 175, 176 Top & Bottom, 178 Bottom Left & Right, 179 Bottom Left & Right, 180 Top & Bottom, 182 Top, Centre, Bottom Left & Right, 184 Top left & Right, Centre & Bottom, 185 Top Left & Right, Bottom, 187, 188 Top, Bottom Left & Right, 189, 190, 192 Top Left & Right, Bottom Left & Right, 194 Left & Right, 196 Top Centre & Bottom, 197 Top, Bottom Left & Right, 208, 209 Top & Bottom, 216 Top & Bottom, 211 Top, Bottom, Left & Right, 212 Bottom, 213 Top & Bottom, 214 Top & Bottom Left.